Language of the Land

An Anthology of Poetry and Nature Writing

Edited by:
Sue Burge, Lesley Mason, Bob Ward and Jonathan Ward

Published in 2025 by All Weathers Press
with the support of Norfolk Wildlife Trust.

© Susanne Anderson, Patrick Barkham, Sue Boag, Jaqueline Bryony, Sue Burge, Adam Curtis, Kathrine Drakley, Annie Giraud, Tina Green, Cornel Howells, Amanda Jane, Tony Langford, Peter Lloyd, Lesley Mason, Maddie McMahon, Sharon Nightingale, Barb Shannon, Barbara Stackwood, Chris Tassell, Heather Tyrrell, Ann Haley Wade, Bob Ward, Jonathan Ward, Jane Wilkinson, Peter Wilson.

The moral and legal rights of all authors and artists to be identified as the authors and/or creators of their work herein have been asserted in accordance with the Copyright, Designs and Patents Act 1988.

ISBN: 978-1-0369-1046-4

All rights reserved. No part of this publication may be reproduced, stored in a retrieval system, or transmitted at any time or by any means electronic, mechanical, photocopying, recording or otherwise without the prior permission of the copyright holder.

Front cover artwork: Barbara Stackwood, based on her original embroidered panel "The Fabric of Cley".

Internal illustrations: Bob Ward.

Poetry & Prose: as shown on the relevant pages.

Printed in Calibri by Micropress Printers, Reydon, Suffolk.

At the Summer Solstice – Heather Tyrrell (see p. 95)

*To all those who have attended a 'Writing Outside' workshop
at Norfolk Wildlife Trust at Cley Marshes,
whether you came once or many times,
in the early days or more recently or both,*

we hold this land in common and all of your words are sacred.

Foreword by Patrick Barkham
(Natural History Writer & President of Norfolk Wildlife Trust)

How does North Norfolk speak to you? A newcomer to this coastline, more familiar with the cliffs, coves and primary colours of the Atlantic edge, might find this low, flat landscape communicating with them in an underwhelming monotone. For here is a place of horizontal lines, few trees and little cosiness. Its muted palette of greys, mauves and muds has none of the peacock-mingled pizzazz of, say, Cornwall.

Spend more than a day here, however, at any time of year, and something shifts and stirs. The sea is a different beast each day and so is the mighty sky, traced with bright filaments of cloud one day and epic billowing towers of cumulus the next. The most spectacular shows come at dawn and dusk. In midsummer, the northern sky glows blue beyond midnight; in midwinter, the sunset seems to last forever, and this epic arena glows pink as skeins of geese come down to roost.

The space and peace seeps into you. The salt air and the cry of lone birds on the marsh is part of a grand holistic treatment that soothes, restores and stimulates. By the end of your sojourn, however long or short it might be, your heart will thud as you realise you have fallen in love. Feel free to become evangelical about it. Like me – hallelujah – you have seen the light. It sometimes takes me a day to come to my senses on Cley Marshes, at Holkham Bay or in the hidden folds of the River Stiffkey, but when I do I remember: this is the best place ever!

The language of this landscape is one where human tongues do not dominate. Here the elements still hold sway, and other species, particularly birds but also marsh plants and intertidal creatures, still thrive. Sapiens shrinks into relative insignificance, which is strangely reassuring, refreshing and galvanising.

The landscape of North Norfolk is a great gift. We may snatch its munificence in weekend breaks or decide to live here more permanently; we may experience it alone or with family and friends, and we may seek out its benefits under the guise of another activity – walking the dog, watching birds, taking photographs, sailing, swimming, cycling, touring.

As well as taking such gifts from this land, we also give back. We may support local causes, or volunteer for conservation groups or simply spread the word about this special place, celebrating it, and joining calls to enhance the vital protections that this landscape enjoys or restore more of it for the species that make their homes here.

We are also moved to create, to bear witness to what's here, to celebrate its special qualities and draw others' attention to it. This coast is famed as a destination for artists, who are enraptured by the light. The peaceful exhilaration we find here drives other creative endeavours too. Jonathan Ward is one of many poets and writers who has found it impossible not to write about North Norfolk. This is the muse at work. We cannot help ourselves!

Through his Cley writing group, Jonathan has helped many others pay close and careful attention to this landscape as well – beginners and experienced writers; people who've written quietly for years without having the courage to share their words; people who've finally got round to unlocking the inner creativity they always hoped they could rediscover. (We were all creatives once, it's just that most of us lose touch with our child genius.)

This anthology is a glorious showcase of the writing and poetry created by those members of the group who have attended since 2021, when we all emerged from the covid pandemic with a revitalised appreciation for the natural world; when we nourished a new thankfulness and a new realisation that local green – and blue – spaces are vitally important not just for our mental and physical wellbeing but for the very continuation of our species.

When William Wordsworth wandered as lonely as a cloud in the Lake District he was actually accompanied by his talented sister, Dorothy, who also wrote brilliantly about their natural world. Whatever the claims of a lone, enraptured poet, words arise from societies. Our lone endeavours are always communal to a certain degree. The writing here is an acknowledgement of that, forged in a supportive community. We writers spark off each other, as well as other species, and the earth, wind and sky around us.

Spending time in a small group outdoors, experiencing, thinking about, and discussing our place and our neighbouring species is a lovely thing to do. It is an act of openness and generosity, and from it stems open and generous writing.

You'll find it in these pages. Scores of ways of looking at the world that we may not have previously considered. Encouraging us to observe more closely, appreciate more fully, and feel more deeply. This anthology is rich in close observation and local distinctiveness. It sings with the spirit of North Norfolk. It also reflects more universal truths about our place in the natural world. Here is a gift, here is a blessing, and here is renewed inspiration for us to step outside, wherever we are, and appreciate anew the world around us. Let's cherish it, together, as we enjoy our moment in this intense, wondrous and oh-so-fleeting dance of life.

Introduction by Jonathan Ward

" ... literature is usually made up of small gatherings in scraps of landscape." Ronald Blythe

My own love of the natural world goes back to childhood walks with my father in The Cotswolds. I still remember those walks around local lanes and paths at different times of the day and in all seasons and all weathers. This, on reflection, is the deepest root and inspiration for the nature writing workshops — Creative Writing Outside — which I began to run for Norfolk Wildlife Trust (NWT) at Cley Marshes in the spring of 2016.

Language of the Land is an anthology of poetry and nature writing by members of the Cley writing group who have attended since the post-lockdown summer of 2021. NWT Cley Marshes, with its commitment to inspiring people to connect with Norfolk's wildlife and wild spaces and to value and care for them, has proved to be an ideal base for this ongoing project.

Looking back, the very first writing walk was to Walsey Hills on April 12, 2016, along the footpath beginning beside Snipe's Marsh on the Cley Reserve which the group quickly began to refer to as The Blackthorn Tunnel. The first poem I received after that first expedition was by Jane Wheeler, an ever-present member of the group in the early years:

blackthorn tunnel

it was as if we were walking into winter

the air changed

so did the light, under

delicate blossom like snow flakes

and beneath, the grim old stems

held long thorns like bayonets.

but the sounds were of spring,

chiffchaff's steady beat

and then loud above

willow warbler's silvery cascade.

Rather fittingly as it turned out, Jane described the piece as 'just an ordering of a communal thought' which acknowledges the shared experience, close observation and discussion that has always been so central to what we do. One of the joys of working in a group is the pooling of knowledge and expertise about what we encounter in nature. It has always been a community project, and a community of writers — 'the Cley writers' — has developed around the meetings. One member of the group introduced us to Jackee Holder's wonderful phrase 'the sacred nature of writing in community' and so it continues to prove.

The format of the workshops is simple: we meet, listen to prompts and examples of nature writing in a variety of forms, such as poems, prose and nature diaries. Then, with notebooks and pens in hand, we set out for a walk and the opportunity to just be outside in the landscape and write. A diversity of responses and forms is welcomed.

I had no idea how long the workshops would continue to run for; but here we are nine years down the line and the sessions are still going from strength-to-strength with an ever-growing pool of writers who attend as life allows. There are annual blocks of seasonal, three-hour workshops and a block of four full Summer Days in July and August.

Frequent writing visits to locations within the Cley Reserve and out to the North Sea have always been central to the workshop programme, but Cley has also served as the hub for our regular trips out to other local landscapes and habitats, such as Bayfield Woods, The River Glaven and Glandford Ford, Salthouse, Blakeney Marshes, the Kelling Heath Drovers' path, the Kelling beach path, local churches and churchyards and Weybourne Cliffs — places which will become familiar as you read this anthology.

The workshops have always been open to beginners and more experienced writers alike — all that is required is an enthusiasm for the natural world and a willingness to be 'open' both to the exercises in the workshops and to what we encounter on our excursions.

We always participate in a prompted seven minute 'free write' and read-round to 'tune in' before setting off to write outside 'in the field'. Sessions end with a final read-round of 'findings' from our walks. I often use phrases like 'the walk is the text', 'foraging for' or 'gathering', 'what will you find today?' We never know what it is we will find, what will take our attention or inspire us — indeed, the location of each walk remains a mystery to the group until the morning of the workshop.

The act of returning to these local places over the years and watching the seasons change has provided a powerful and moving stimulus — the group finds great significance in rituals of return, such as our visits to an old boat, slowly decaying on the edge of the Blakeney saltmarsh, the snowdrops at Bayfield and visits to favourite trees with which people have formed deep relationships — observing them, telling stories, remembering and listening in.

Many places have become sacred to us where we gather to read our words aloud: the clearing in the woods by the fallen rowan tree, the stone circle behind the shingle ridge, the field edge by the midden and the skylark field or at the edge of the sea.

At the heart of the writing outside experience is finding time to be still, to pay attention, to notice, being patient and open to where we are taken in our minds and writing ... and to share. There are no rules as to what 'type' or form of text we produce — risk and experiment is encouraged — and what each individual chooses to write about is of the day and of the moment: details of flora and fauna, bird sightings, history, the changing seasons and weather, the light, childhood memory, care and concern for the natural world, climate change, wake up calls for action and the heartlands of more deeply personal journeys and wellbeing.

There have been many writers involved in the Cley sessions over the years, but the idea of producing an anthology finally gained momentum in the aftermath of the pandemic — those sessions I came to refer to as 'Returning to Cley' and 'Immersed in Cley'. A new, enhanced spirit of emotional openness and vulnerability pervaded the group as we set out on those first post-pandemic walks in July 2021. That summer, as we walked out together from the visitor centre to locations in and alongside the Cley Reserve, there was an overwhelming sense of gratitude and delight to be back in a group, sharing time in nature and hearing other people's voices, words and experiences.

Over the years, the group has regularly put up a display of work at Cley and given a public performance of works produced during the latest season — these have always been a pleasure to attend and a true celebration. They have included a wonderful array of material including songs. In this sense the spirit of sharing words has been present at Cley since 2016.

There have also been further off-shoots, such as photographs, art works, a whole range of home-made pamphlets and artists' books, plus a series of broadsheet publications called 'Inside Writing Outside', produced by Bob Ward, a member of the group since the earliest sessions.

What you will find in *Language of the Land* is a sampling of the work of the group. It is our way of sharing our responses to Cley and the surrounding landscape with a wider readership. We hope you enjoy, and are inspired by, what you find in its pages. You may even feel encouraged to join us in the workshops or to attend the regular readings at the Visitor Centre at Cley, or simply to share in the process of heading out for a walk with a notebook and your own thoughts, open to what you encounter.

CONTENTS

Susanne Anderson   1
Single Yellow Poppy
Seabed
Snowdrops, February 2024

Sue Boag   4
Marsh Harrier
Winter

Jaqueline Bryony   6
My Soul Place
Two Sisters
The Visitors

Sue Burge   13
What the geese mean
If this were a fairy tale
Snow Queen
Field Notes taken standing in Glandford Ford
Saltmarsh

Adam Curtis   18
Time for Rooks
The Woodland Wren
Winter Snowdrops

Kathrine Drakley   23
Autumn's Golden Cloak
Desert by the Sea
Give Thanks and Gratitude
Snipe's Pool
Fisher Widow's Prayer

Annie Giraud   28
Seal-Dogs
Filigree Dragon
Hag
Gold
MAEUM: SEA STORM 13

Tina Green   35
The Screen
The River Glaven in January
Bayfield Woods: Autumn – 10 steps, 10 steps apart
Rap to the Weed
For Juliet

Cornel Howells   40
The Kelling Heath Oak
Brief Candles
A Cloud Passes Over the Sun

Amanda Jane   44
The Old Boat
Light
Marshland
The Churchyard
Autumn Thought

Tony Langford   51
When I Am Among the Trees
Cley Calling
Nature Will
Intersection
I Hear Noises

Peter Lloyd   56
Lost and Found in Nature
The Mystery of the Sea
Robin's wreck on Blakeney Point
By the Glaven
Layers of Sound: On a winter walk to Blakeney Marshes

Lesley Mason   61
Marsh Whispers
Back to Walsey Hills
Oak
Blow-ins

Maddie McMahon   **66**
Wood Woman
Fallen Leaf
Renaissance
The Sun Comes out Eventually

Sharon Nightingale   **73**
My North Sea

Barb Shannon   **78**
Blue Light
Summer Solstice Walks
RAW – Field Notes
Harvest
Becoming plant life

Barbara Stackwood   **85**
This is the sea – Today
Sea Urchin
Immersed in Cley
Steps in Cley
Leaving the Flatland

Chris Tassell   **90**
Glandford Glimmers
A Brief Encounter in Bayfield Woods
Cley East Beach on the dunes, 2021
Cley East Beach, 2023
Coastwise

Heather Tyrrell   **95**
At the Summer Solstice
I won't be quiet!
Retrospective

Ann Haley Wade   **99**
Cormorant
Miranda by the Sea
Old Path in Spring
Mother Courage in Salthouse

Bob Ward 104
Dragonflies
Saltmarsh Creek
Along the Way
Going to Seed
Language of the Land

Jonathan Ward 111
Patience
A Gift

Jane Wilkinson 116
Funeral Ceremony for a Dogfish
Down Reading Room Loke and straight on to
Father in a Summer Wood

Peter Wilson 121
Finding a Whale
April 1992 – Inspired by Wiveton Down
The Rabbit Bank

Appendix 129

Authors 131

Acknowledgements 135

Illustrations by Bob Ward

Horned Poppy on a Shingle Beach	*next page*
Paying Attention	11
Breakwater Meets the Sea	33
Winter Branches	49
Which Way is South?	71
Hogweed Horizon	83
Reeds Whispering to the Wind	109
Quizzical Owl	127

Susanne Anderson

Single Yellow Poppy

This limbo-lunar land
of salt, stone, sand,
long-crushed limpets and red
lichens, alive, amongst rusted
metal and dead tree-arms, twisted
to sun-bleached eels
is where, alone, I spread
my yellow-pale dress and flail.

Susanne Anderson

Seabed

You cover your bed in a white lace sheet
and I wait for you on the shore,
watching you sleep,
turning and glistening, twisting, grey-greens,
trying to reach me in your dreams.

Then, you wake with a huge rasping yawn,
of a thousand saws,
rake closer, grasping, catching, glassy claws,
lifting, shallowing, swallowing,
your ebb and scroll, blue-hued flow,
gun-melted grey,
sheet tattered to foam and spray,
and I'm snatched up, in a high
ride, low writhe and thrown,
back to land, to dry in the sand.

For this is how we roll,
forever, together,
you the sea, and I, the stone.

Susanne Anderson

Snowdrops, February 2024

I dropped a cup, warming milk for morning coffee, and it smashed to pieces, shattered to shards in white spreading foam.
It was a portent. Later, I saw you, Galanthus, your soft, white cup dropping, spilling into the grey winter river, but it seemed that, at the very last minute, you clutched the mossy bank with your thin, green arms, and saved yourself from drowning, face down.

Anytime, soon, heavy snowfall could bend your face to the earth, tear your fragile pale flesh, crush out your light.
You know that, but you saved yourself for today.
And no milk spilt.
No crying.

Marsh Harrier
24.01.23

Magnificence
Holding
Frozen moment
Spellbound, waiting
Watching
Transfixed and Trans-fixer

Diver
Perfect ten
Vanishes
Frozen seconds
No escape
Rises, life sustained.

Sue Boag

Winter

The sun holds in its hands the bone of winter, smiling, gracing us with its presence, giving us permission to hope. Hope that spring will arrive, that life will renew, that summer will shine, and that the new autumn will once again prepare us for another year.

But to hope for future seasons before the sun allows winter to settle its cloak across the land, is to miss what our eyes can see, what our ears can hear. To miss the warmth held in our hearts that keeps us going at the early dying of a winter's day.

The sparkling drops of ice on a frosted pond, the small shoots of renewal held in cold fastness, waiting for the moment to throw away their chains. Animals in winter coats, warm in the knowledge of protection, backs turned from ice and rain in disdain. The early birds returning from distant shores, the awakening of sleeping mammals. The winter sea sharing its mood as it shouts towards the shore, promising us better things to come as the sleepy sun hits the crest of a wave.

All these and more, held in icy winter thrall, show us that life still stirs, life still moves, the future is in this moment. If only, if only, we stop, breathe, and look.

Jaqueline Bryony

My Soul Place

The sea is my soul place.
The myriad different sounds,
 like chants, beckon me for worship.

We meet at a regular
time and place, just like
a congregation. There is

no order of service, we are
the non-conformists.
We know what to do,

without explanation. Our main
event is not bread and wine
but coffee and cake.

We too, share in a mystical
peace. Our daily sermons
range from garlic to ghosts,

camel's milk to the Wim Hof
method. Our prayer time
is full of gratitude,

many thanks and songs of
praise. Ah, but do not
be misled, we struggle

with chaos, grief and pain.
Some are sick, one faces
eviction and tomorrow

another has an operation.
You see, we often
swim in tears. But

when we are finished we
end our time with complete
immersion, our baptism of fire.

Jaqueline Bryony

Two Sisters

What stories you could tell
With your gnarled arms
and broken branches.

You are so tall and
graceful as you age,
and to me, entirely beautiful.

Two sisters standing side by side
arms outstretched
reaching for each other.

Oh sister, parts of you
are dead and other parts
are only half alive.

What happened to us?
Broken by storms,
weighed down by grief.

Your branches reach the floor,
they are heavy still
with autumn leaves

Your beauty rises
and greets the sun,
your bark is stripey

like sand on the sea shore.
There is nothing here to
compare with your beauty.

Oh sister, how did we arrive
at this terrible place
of muddle and dark?

I miss the beauty of
your face. I miss
Your humour and your grace.

Now, like the trees, we are grey
and splintered. Pitted with age
and longing to begin us again.

Jaqueline Bryony

The Visitors

Along they came, looking for fun the whole
weekend. They flew along the empty roads,
too busy to notice the beauty in the landscape,
as they hurtled on to other delights.

They raced along the narrow roads and missed
the riches hiding in the reeds. They longed for
other things like feasting, champagne
and dancing all night long.

But some pleasures are more simple,
like the geese in flight, or an egret
edging along the muddy bank.
A wading redshank, or the curlew's call.

Those Bentley Boys knew how to party,
with their two-tone Brogues and wicked smiles.
Their expensive toys and elegant clothes,
they were definitely out to impress.

Perhaps they thought, "we're on track,
free from officials and rules of the road."
But Grandpa, they didn't know,
that you once drove a Bentley,
and held the record, from Ely to Cambridge.

You raced on other tracks and never slowed down,
even as you sped along the bypass, worrying us all.
But keeping records or racing roads,
could never compare to the beauty
and pleasure we shared that day.

Sue Burge

What the geese mean

I am often waiting for wild geese
to write their unruly Vs across the sky

with a hundred thousand wingbeats
it's not proper winter unless... I say

but what does it matter if the sky
that's holding all the world's blue

over the saltmarshes is unpunctuated?
Because here are swans, dreaming

their slow white dreams; lapwing
unfurling their long scroll of banter;

and here's the cold, still sea, keeping
its blue-grey secrets close.

And because not seeing the geese
means I can come out another day

and not think about all the other things
that make the sky darken.

Sue Burge

If this were a fairy tale

there would be ancient woods bordering this marshland
a deep dark once upon a time

brambles, briars and swathes of sea buckthorn
would shout *keep out* instead of wire's cold tug

the curlew overhead would be an enchanted prince
wielding his beaky sword in readiness

tasked to tremolo his song a thousand times
before the spell can break

there would be a quest: seven seas to push back
in seven days; no villains to conjure floodwaters & north-westerlies

the hero's pockets would contain talismans: milky sea glass,
the parched seedcases of honesty, a hag-stone for his bride

warblers would weave his shirt from the reeds' whispery heads
he would learn the calm magic of fox bark and grasshopper click

there would be one princess to rescue instead of a whole world
waking from a hundred years of soot

if this were a fairy tale
there would be a happily ever after

Sue Burge

Snow Queen

Trapped in her shadowy room, Mary Queen of Scots embroiders snowdrops on taut linen. *Fleurs de perce-neige,* she whispers, remembering the pale gardens of childhood, when they would push through the hard earth, insistent as a stiletto blade — pretty February maids all in a row. How one day she took pity on them, the splay of their ragged heads, sleet-punched, lolling, their little hearts nearly broken; how she brought them indoors, how the servants hid their eyes — *poisonous little corpses in their battered shrouds.*

At night she hears the rush of water, a nearby river — or is it rain? She cannot distinguish horizontal, vertical. Does not know which way up she is in this slow cold world where she endlessly dreams of blood on snow, snow on blood.

Sue Burge

Field Notes taken standing in Glandford Ford (River Glaven) 9 August 2022

the Glaven is wearing sequins today
a moth drowns face down in the gold

a black dog sleek and handsome as Shuck
howls with water-joy

children shout of monsters   I dream
of otters   old coins trapped under stones

blackberries ripen over the water
willow-herb bows its rosy head

nearby cows squint through veils of flies
eavesdrop on the ford's cool words

a white feather floats past a leaf —
waterlogged   blackened

this quiet stream once a great river
hymns its unassuming self to sea

Sue Burge

Saltmarsh

We came for the loneliness
to lose our minds in tall skies
cleansed by the reliability of tides.

We came to be unboundaried
unmoored; to be sculpted by wind
hollowed out, refuelled.

We came to rewrite our stories
wet our feet in sly waters
turn our tame blood wild.

We came for the old knowledge —
mud's remembrance, skylark's litany
sea kale's candid nourishment.

We came for the water, the silverways
and if the water comes for us
that's okay, we'll stay.

Adam Curtis

Time for Rooks

We overlook a Rookery.

The conservation area in our market town protects an acre of woodland and the proud trees stand tall of the red tile rooftops. The Sycamore, Oak and Lime protected from disturbance by dense Holly, is where they roost and nest. As dusk approaches, someone in our home will hear the first *Cragghhh* and make the call. *"Rook o'clock."* We leave the house, flocking together in the garden and look for their arrival. *"Here they come."* They tumble into our hearts, descending overhead as they terminate their flight in the woods. Hundreds, a thousand, maybe more, are swelled by as many Jackdaws – the diminutive corvid cousins with piercing blue eyes and silver sheen to their mantles.

Rooks gathering at dusk aren't united in movement like a murmuration of Starlings, moving as if one. Nor do they perform the breathtaking, light catching swirls of wading birds that play with the warm evening sun to catch and bounce and reflect the warm light. No, not the Rooks and Jackdaws. They fill the air more with gothic melancholy as they silhouette against the pale slate evening sky. This is our homely, daily spectacle and it fills our lives with the joy of nature's rhythm.

They spend their days dispersed around the agricultural landscape and come directly together at dusk. The credit for the expression *'as the crow flies',* is stolen from the Rook. Standing beneath them, they are gregarious and amplify their call above the din of the crowd – a rowdy London pub. Murder, Mob, Horde, Parliament, Clamour, Clattering. These are the collective nouns for Corvids.

Maligned by Alfred Hitchcock who portrayed them as sinister and foreboding, alluding to the bad omens we hold for Corvids in folk lore. The Rook's bill, sharp and stout, could peck an eyeball from the skull of a suffering beast but its use is to probe soft worms from hard earth. Bygone Rooks were thought a pest to farmers who built misnamed scarecrows.

The nursery rhyme '*Four and twenty blackbirds*' was also stolen from the Rook. In the past the fledglings were shot in mid-May when sufficiently plump for a pie yet too young to fly. They nourished us and so Rooks were also positive omens in folklore. It was bad luck for a rookery to be abandoned – imminent death of the landowner and poor fortune for the community.

Living beside Rooks and Jackdaws is life affirming. Today they are recognised as helping the farmer, mitigating grain consumption by removing more crop damaging grubs from the soil. I love that they form lifelong pair bonds and, taking time to look, I see groups of two above our marital home.

Rooks are not to be overlooked.

Adam Curtis

The Woodland Wren

Familiar to those who love an arboreal adventure, I entered the woods and felt a sense of belonging. Footsteps walked in the cultural setting of fables, folklore and fairy tales. Footsteps walked with Hansel and Gretel, the babes in the woods and even the Gruffalo whose journey starts *'A mouse took a stroll in a deep dark wood'.*

I check the map. Woodlands obscure our view. The distance we can see in dense forest can be just a tree's length or two. No miles-long view or vista, no big blue skies, we can't see the wood for the trees from within. Woodlands hold a place in our psyche and sub-conscious on life's journey. Our time spent in woodland requires trusting the route through a dark place. Reaching our destination is assured if we keep to the path through the woods. But stray from the beaten track.

As I walk, I forget life's journey and relax into the moment. I stop searching for the way, my feet follow the track and my senses heighten. It doesn't take long to tune into woodland smells, sights and sounds. It's autumn and the Foxgloves' flowers have topped out, the Woodsage scent is spent and mixed groups of tits twitter in unison as they feed in the tree tops. Safety in numbers, familiar friends. Blue Tit, Great Tit, Coal Tit and the Long-Tailed Tit. To listen is bliss enough but given time (and binoculars) there's a chance of a Goldcrest, Firecrest or maybe a Lesser Spotted Woodpecker.

Then punching through air, the *churr* of a Wren. They punch far above their weight which is only a feather's weight heavier than the Goldcrest, though shorter and dumpier. They are an abundant breeding bird, yet their behaviour makes them difficult to spot. Their scientific name is *Troglodytes troglodytes* – the 'troglodyte' or cave dweller derived from the Greek meaning 'to creep into holes', which describes the Wren as it searches in scrub for insects, in crevices to roost and cavities to nest.

Creeping into holes, Wrens feel secure, safe and sheltered. Creeping into woodlands, we feel sheltered from wind, rain and sun, sheltered and safe from the rigours of life's journeys. Respite belongs in woodlands, perhaps more so than any other landscape or habitat. We need trees, in abundance. Woods are three-dimensional; they tower over us, entering a woodland is immersive and to descend into woodland is to experience belonging and safety. To be 'tree-hugged'.

I lived in a woodland house, with the bedrooms set partially into the roof. The tired holey soffits lay level with my line of sight when lying in bed. At dusk Wrens would fleet up into the soffit to communally roost for warmth in winter.

Occasionally I would find one in the house having crept too deep into the lofty cavern and found a way through the airing cupboard, the door left ajar. A foolish Wren that spends too long and goes too far into the cave. In Aesop's Fables when the birds competed to be king the little Wren hitched a lift on the back of the Eagle and flew just that bit higher! – Wisdom triumphing over strength on life's journey.

Adam Curtis

Winter Snowdrops

Snowdrops are her favourite flower; she tells me this every year when the first green leaves appear in early February. She has other favourite flowers of course. Following in the floral procession: Primroses, Cowslips, Bluebells, Hawthorn, Ox-eye Daisies, Foxgloves …..

With Snowdrops I sense the joy she experiences as the promise of a winter blossom starts to appear. The picture she messaged to me when the first glimpse of bridal white appeared in the yet unfurled leaf. Simplicity and purity of the flower.

I care not for the oversized, misshapen flowers of the garden cultivars selected to show off and glamourise what is perfect and naturally pretty.

A valentine walk snatched between showers. Winter birds still feeding in the treetops, their song now changing to spring. I hear an unfamiliar call and I search with binocular vision, half catching sight of a Brambling. Frustratingly elusive.

She called me to admire the Snowdrops, gathered now in abundance. I awaken from my futile midwinter quest of a rare sighting, hidden too deep.

She is *my* February fair maiden turning me away from winter's folly and now pointing me to look outward from the forest shadow. She beckons me to not just hear, but to see the summer's first lark, filling our sky with sunny richness.

Snowdrops are her favourite flower. My winter blossom.

Kathrine Drakley

Autumn's Golden Cloak

I turn from iron road to silken sea,
to thread my way through soft bronze
      reed-filled marsh leading west to east.
          I spin 360 degrees;
              to worship; become one with this land
          I weave a cloak of whispering emerald,
      feathered with fluttering bronzed seed-heads.
    enhanced by golden sun and opal sky;
washed with strokes of white.
    as I walk, my cloak picks up purple of aster,
        carmine of samphire, yellow of poppy.
          As a goodbye to summer
             the sky is full of birdsong;
        swallows dart and dive;
      weaving their own patterns
of sound and colour.
Autumn colours of kestrel;
      marsh harrier hover; then spin away
          to rise and loop;
              like warp and weft
                  on the loom above.
          This saltmarsh
        that joins land to sea
    in a seamless pattern
of rainbow light
      a memory to hold
           through the darker days of winter.

Kathrine Drakley

Desert by the Sea

A shingle garden of colour
greens, greys, reds, yellows and white
horned poppies, birds foot trefoil
stonecrops, sea campion and grasses,
all clinging to life,
surviving
battering seas and raging winds.
Today,
hear the skylark rising,
linnet and redshank calling,
stonechat and wheatear foraging,
ringed plover nesting.
This is an oasis in the wilderness,
a place of stark beauty,
solace and solitude,
here in nature's garden of cultivars.

Kathrine Drakley

Give Thanks and Gratitude

Shamanic Teachings from The Sioux Nation

All life is sacred; treat all beings with respect.

Let us now give thanks

for this winter wild place

home to migrants,

wigeon, teal, plover

pink footed geese

and many others

in need of food,

shelter and safety

in this shrinking world.

Enjoy life's journey but leave no traces behind.

Kathrine Drakley

Snipe's Pool

sparkles in icy silence

nothing moves

but sunbeams

skating the surface

in golden grace

leaving swirls

across the ice

lone buzzard

glides above

as he returns

to his tree top eyrie

now exposed

what secret does he hold

the secret of survival in a winter landscape

Kathrine Drakley

Fisher Widow's Prayer

I look to you St Nicholas to help me in my prayers.

I plead with you, my child.

Look west my child, look west,
Look south my child, look south.

I implore you, my child.

Do not look north, do not look north
Nor east, nor east.

I pray for you, my child.

Look inland for a safer trade, shepherding,
Apprenticed to a kindly master.

I plead with you, my child.

Do not look seaward
To a cruel and fickle mistress.

I implore you, my child.

It is a harsh, crippling life,
Following the silver darlings.
I pray for you my child, do not break a mother's heart.

Annie Giraud

Seal-Dogs

A leatherneck aquaplanes and plunges through spilling
breakers as North Sea rolls ashore in plurals;
    over the shingle bank
        a million reed sisters whisper secrets.
        Two vivacious dandelions burn oil into Autumn.
An inquisitive promenader treads water a pebble's throw
from taut fishing lines;
    over the shingle bank
        wigeons commandeer a tar-black scrape,
        doodling trails with tails a-flicking.
A corpulent beauty of patent leather skis through surf,
performs a double twist and half pike;
    over the shingle bank
        a rush of twitchers with bins and scopes
        focuses on a wheatear, adrift and alone.
A perfectly balanced trampolinist apes the swing and spring
of flags on the buoys of crab pots;
    over the shingle bank
        rough tufts stand strictly to attention
        like an army of Hergé's Tintins.
A flash of black-silver and a graceful illusionist appears
with glossy binoculars trained on shore;
    over the shingle bank
        a weary sun stains reeds with tinctures of pink.
        A swirl of geese bark and bay to touchdown.
A rolling turbine gathers speed and is soon a distant dot,
cruising the silkie road without a passport;
    over the shingle bank
        two-stroke crows are engine revving.
        Fast red-metal flickers on the coast road.

Annie Giraud

Filigree Dragon

I can see your bones.
Every one.
Indigo.
Pewter.
Hawthorn hedge, you are splendid!
Clouds bow low to you, tumbling over folds
in their voluminous stonewashed greys.
Your thorny skeleton scribbles against sky as strong
and bold as Buckingham Palace gates.
On the rounded head of Walsey Hills,
you are fashioned into a stiff Mohican.
Further away, your cousins have linked vertebrae into
a single whaleback.
Perhaps you were once enslaved by nearby marsh,
until you escaped and laboured up this hill.
You are the Filigree Dragon of Walsey Hills.
Artist!
Truth is, someone planted you.
For convenience.
Windbreak.
You split the flint-pimpled acres.
Forced to adapt, now squat and round shouldered,
you fend off North Sea's disfiguring winds.
Up here today on this old trail,
the air pecks at my cheeks rather kindly
and there is a burst of affection from sun.
You stand stiffly to attention, ready to spring.
It will not be long.
It's a new year, after all.

Annie Giraud

Hag

I happenstanced upon a stump,
a once oak, contorted,
grimacing in dance of death,
charred, electrocuted.
Wading ankle deep
through its discharged history
of cinnamon crisps and curled cheroots,
I gazed upon a witchery.
Rickety ramparts, dented armour,
thickets of crazed leather
now draped upon a squatter's back,
smug with her seized treasure.
Beneath four suppurating pustules
Hag bulged an eye to charm;
clutching begging bowl of canker,
thrust out arthritic arm.
Legs oozing ulcerations,
gangrenous toes turned to coal,
inside her exposed rib cave
I found a splintered soul.

Annie Giraud

Gold

Barley bows
A simple obeyance
as though prayer might hasten growth.
Ears,
not of the hearing kind.
Ears,
not weighted down
by gemstone piercings,
silver, ruby or aquamarine,
but laden with twenty suckling grains,
individually and meticulously gift wrapped
in crisp husk
and defended
by whiskers that are as mean as stilettoes.
Ears,
cleaving to skinny sky-stalks
whose defined segments
look ready to fold into spyglasses.
Before the harvester clouds this field in dust and
the maltster makes his claim,
the gilder will arrive
to finalise this galleon's glory.
Raise your tankards to a fine brew!

Annie Giraud

MAEUM: SEA STORM 13

Denim drifter. Surly sky-goth.
Scoundrel in cheap tie-dyed T-shirt.
Million-dollar blockbuster trailing across the firmament.
    Flamenco dancer's oiled hair in a bun.
    Marie Antoinette's bouffant without a fixing pin in sight.
    Untamed ringlets without my daughter's smile.
Maeum drops low. Haunting.
Obliterates the horizon, howling like a wolf.
Camouflages turbines in porpoise skin shirts.
Spins crab pot buoys into whirling dervishes.
Fluffs wave crests into candyfloss and two second snowmen.
Fleetingly, a sun-struck, red-lipstick ship is star of the show.
    John Williams raises his baton, chases E.T. across the sky.
    Camille Saint-Saens' Organ Concerto forgets to brake.
    Trumpets steal the Magic Flute; Mozart loses his temper.
Suddenly, (yes, there is often a suddenly) ...
Sunbeams split Maeum's raindrops into gifts:
    Remembrance poppies,
    Juicy tangerines,
    Sauntering sunflowers,
    Mushy peas,
    Strutting peacocks,
    Blueberry pies,
    Fearless violets.

We are the cliff-top watchers. Gripped. We dab at tears. Say nothing.
After the show, we nod at each other in a satisfied way.

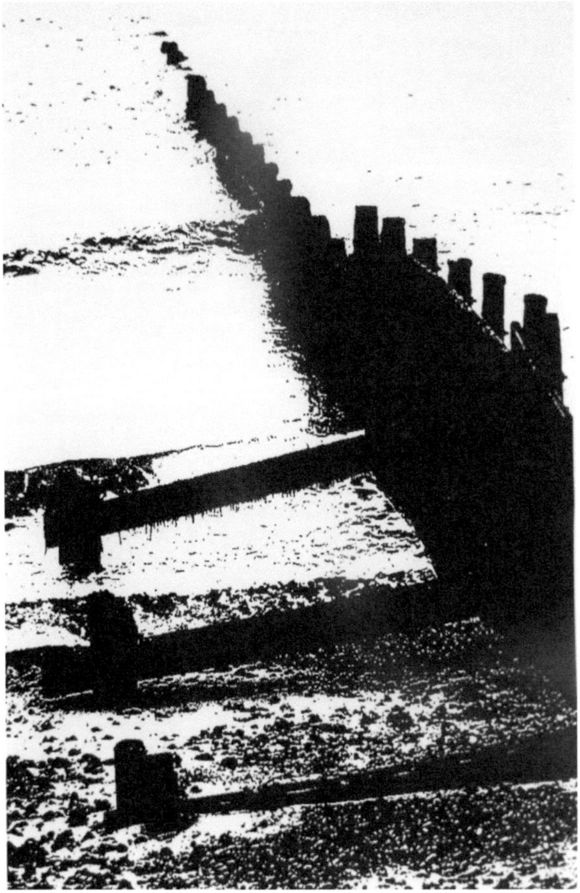

Tina Green

The Screen

Is it improper to stare at beautiful
Creatures through a screen?
Unaware, with no need of modesty
The swans stretch their necks,
Hold their ground and look around.
Now worrying their beaks amongst
Eider-down beneath their wings.
And then outstretched
In a private lazy yawn.
The swaying reeds screen me
Allowing but disconnected forms,
My impertinent scent
Taken by the breeze.

Tina Green

The River Glaven in January

You do not trip over The Glaven in Winter.
It is the eel in the landscape, bright as quicksilver,
Radiant amongst the dull left-over sedge,
Resplendent as a meadow serpent,
Glinting wave-scales slipping forward.

But come closer its outline is diffuse.
Water-logged reeds sit in quiet pools,
Kept company by the season's early gnats,
Yet water is drawn imperceptibly towards
The slippery current as mud gives way to chalk.

Listen low and you will hear the first murmurings
Of dynamic flow, of the push against pebbles
Against stems, of water joining water,
Drowned out now by the swish of spent
Willowherb and the cry of the crows.

Walk along the bank, sun on your back,
Sun on the bark of trees, shadows of both
And the *eel's* emergent power speaks,
Speeding over the side-drain
Newly white with exciting intent.

Tina Green

Bayfield Woods: Autumn
10 steps, 10 steps apart

Dusky pink mushrooms issue an invitation to
Come close and marvel at their perfect gills.

Tremulous vestiges of bracken
Stalk through the leaf-litter.

Look up to the yellow and green canopy from the
Mossy saddle at the oaks' bifurcation.

Breezes urge papery leaves to take courage
And fall.

Wispy midges float ever upwards as
Long tailed tits dart amongst the trees.

Pale light, casting no shadows holds the
Echo of a buzzard's call.

An empty chestnut case,
The open mouth of a terrestrial anemone.

An offering of fallen leaves lies in a
Bark curl of silver-birch.

Step back on a puff ball and witness
A ceremonial exhalation of new life.

Kick up the bronzed leaves, inhale and feel glad.

Tina Green

Rap to the Weed

Rose   Bay   Willow   Herb
Four   Stamens   Four   Sepals
Four   Stigmas   Four   Petals
Rose   Bay   Willow   Herb

Rose   Bay   Willow   Herb
Thin   Pod   Elong   Gated
Silken Seeds Feather Freighted
Rose   Bay   Willow   Herb

Rose   Bay   Willow   Herb
Bomb   Weed   Fire   Weed
Rail   Weed   Moth   Weed
Rose   Bay   Willow   Herb

Rose   Bay   Willow   Herb
Names   Become   a   Mantra
Four   Vier   Quattro   Quatre
Rose   Bay   Willow   Herb

Tina Green

For Juliet

Juliet loved it here, running
Along the edge between sea
And land, dashing between
Tongues of foam.

I brought her a bunch of
Sea lavender
Twisted together with
Raffia.

She refused morphine
She wanted a clear head
She said.

We all visited and she asked
After our families,
Despite her pain.

The mauve on the windowsill
Opposite her bed had no
Chance to fade, as she did.

Her last memories of the sea
She took with her.

Cornel Howells

The Kelling Heath Oak
Hundreds of years in the making
From my perch on the sandy bank
I look down on you, winking
You too will pass, as they all pass.

And what about me you ask.

As a hedgerow tree
Woodsmen took their axe to me
But each cut made me harder
My bole wider, callouses thicker
Until I turned to stone.

The woodsman went away to war
Which war was that?
Alas, I cannot recall
There have been so many
Returning, he wearily let me be.

The great storm of Defoe renown
Barely ruffled the twigs in my crown
I slumbered through many a great frost
When lesser trees were split asunder
I survived the lightning bolt
Which left others half dead at a stroke.

Old as I may be
Arthritically misshapen and back bent
On stirring in spring
I hoist pennants of green and gold
Into the wide blue sky.

And always the murmur of the sea.

Cornel Howells

Brief Candles

Darkness. Fitful lightning reveals a tumultuous sea. Sea from horizon to horizon. Only sea.

There is no witness. No one. Just sea and sky in violent commotion.

Grey light comes.

I am vapour; risen from the sea.

My long journey begins.

Great cold. I am entombed. A sea frozen in time. The wind whips across the tundra sending dust and ice particles spiralling into the air.

Night. The Aurora. Pale green curtains of light draped across the northern sky. Stars, fierce, dancing in the ice blue light. Comets complete their heavenly orbit again and again. Flaring. Brief candles that no one sees.

People come. They raise me up as a church on this glacial mound, crafted from my stone and flint. I have looked out over this patchwork of village, shoreline, marsh, and heath for almost a millennium. I have watched the affairs of humankind, their constant coming and going. I have heard their talk, mostly of the sea.

And it is to the sea that I look now. I feel its pull.

The sea is coming to reclaim me.

Cornel Howells

A Cloud Passes Over the Sun

Scientists were warning us on the news this morning that we face the prospect of a world without insects. Loss of habitat and climate change, the usual culprits are to blame.

Actual loss evokes powerful negative emotions in us. The prospect of loss is manageable and therefore less urgent. It can somehow be tidied away for another day.

Those of us who are saddened by the thought of a world depleted of wildlife, which is polluted, overcrowded and climatically unstable, are impotent in the face of this threat. Words are rendered sterile and individual restraint is overwhelmed by a tidal wave of human consumption.

These feelings nag at me as I set out along the sunken lane by the sea on this fine early spring day. The decrepitude and decay of winter is finally giving way to the quickening green shoots of spring. Shrunken rose hips, ivy berries and the tired thatch of grass are the last vestiges of the old season's passing. Time to look ahead to the arrival of the first migrant birds, the shimmering new leaf growth and the successive waves of white blossom cascading through the countryside.

Legions of alexanders are already marching along the hedge banks. The fresh green leaves of cow parsley, arum lily, cleavers and nettles abound. A chaffinch has flown into the top of an old hawthorn to give a burst of his spring song. Extrovert hares are romping along the field hedges. The tiny red starry hazel flowers have joined the yellow male catkins and pollination begins.

There can come a moment though, even on the finest of spring days, when all colour and meaning drains away and we are alone in a melancholy, featureless world. I sense this most keenly on early spring days when a stray cloud passes over the sun and a breeze arises, sending the dead leaves on the woodland floor scurrying. It suggests the precariousness of the season and possibly of human existence itself.

Is this anomic feeling a throwback to the time when we were engaged in a daily battle of survival in the natural world? We now believe we have tamed nature, that we are the masters now!

But with the apocalyptic predictions of scientists now rivalling those of the science fiction writers of my youth, it is sobering to reflect that nature is completely indifferent to our stewardship of the planet. It will make do. If we wish to rescue the natural world from a catastrophe of our own making, then the time for fine words and wildlife initiatives is past. The human race needs to radically reduce its global footprint and start now.

I fear this cloud will not pass.

Amanda Jane

The Old Boat

Slowly disappearing vanishing with tide and time

History is held within this vessel with its slowly rotting frame

A sad sight sombre in its mood perhaps once blue

An empty shell with its ribs on show skeletal

Fragile not complete laid bare for all to see

Splintered and rubbed clean by pounding of the wind and sea

Sitting almost still battered and broken

But not yet lost to time and tide

Amanda Jane

Light

Sweeping rays form and catch as the autumn morning grows.

Casting shadows in hazy streams with weightless gleams

Beaming a fair and constant flow of radiant and often blinding light

A rich glare cloudless and clear so vivid

Animated beacons of light strobing from the sky

Filtering into the unseen blazing like wildfire

Sharp and contrasting swathes of fluorescent sheens.

Not only cloaking but powerfully provoking thought

Elements radiate they ignite the senses and vision

Sweeping the landscape from a dreamscape

Flowing travelling with the light vibrant silhouettes visible

Casting of images uncontrollable in the ever-changing light

Amanda Jane

Marshland

Shape-shifting paths and tracks

Forever snaking tapering gaps

Filling pockets pools and cracks

Textures of loamy silty sandbanks

Always adjusting grooves and ruts

Traces and trails erased

With continuous changing lines

It will never be defined

Amanda Jane

The Churchyard

Fragments of time remain chipped away by memories of old

Broken headstones lie flat and out of place

Age has smoothed away so many names

The past and present are mixed in a plotted order

Thick outer walls of flint and brick

Lichen covered stone above bone

Standing to attention generation after generation

The collection begins at the great columned gates

A knowing that we all have the same fate

Many welcoming spirits protect their last resting place

Amanda Jane

Autumn Thought

Gaggling geese gather

Glorious giants gossiping

Gifted GPS guided

Great ganders grazing

Graceful groups gathering

Gentle goslings glimmering

Generations growing grounding

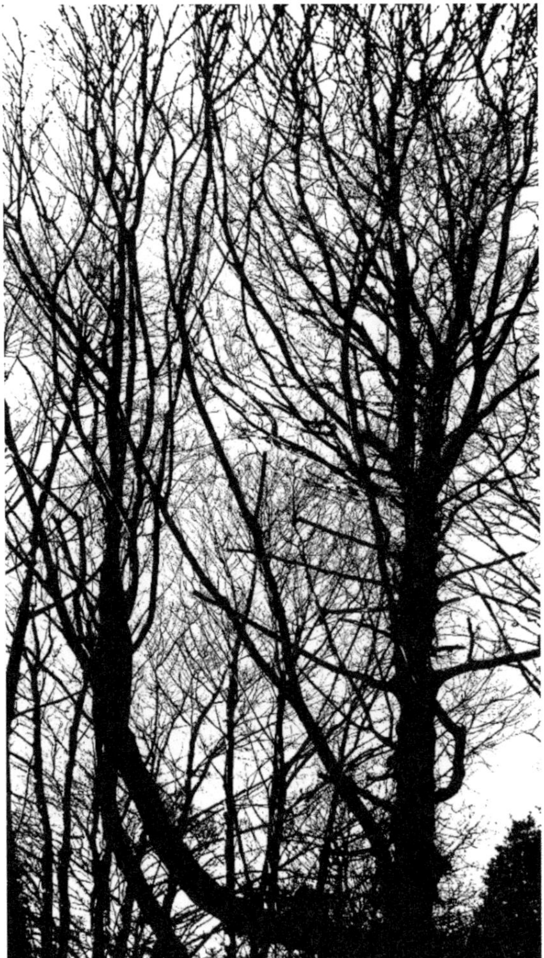

Tony Langford

When I Am Among the Trees
After Mary Oliver

When I am among the trees
And they are among me
We are as one
And embrace each other
In a natural way
And in nature together
Leaving aside the noise
And cares of the World
The drum of disenchantment
Disappears
Replaced by
Quiet murmuring
And the hum
Of contentment

Tony Langford

Cley Calling*

Cley calling, stories unfolding
The sound of diesel engines turning
Grinding tracks harshly send stones churning
The man driving, cold, with cigarette burning
Boats lie dormant, await moving

Crab pots piled high, one against another
Resembling a honeycomb, minus the honey
The scene reminiscent of times gone by
Men working with the Sea, working against the Sea
Always with respect and awe of the Sea

A boat being moved, the *Stanley Allen*
LN9 its number, Tactile 19 on its side
Registered at Lynn, but at Wells resides,
Winching it to a trailer, "Are you local?" I enquired
"Yes, we are," Richard emphatically replied

Young men with a mission, preserving the old ways
The urge from within unrelenting, unwavering
The rewards often meagre, the efforts unchanging
Connected to their heritage in ways unsaid
"So few of us left," almost a lament

A phrase often used by the NWT in their outreach programmes

Tony Langford

Nature Will

The seasons come, the seasons go, we hope them to beguile
But changing scenes, before unseen, create a different sight
We hope for more, for certainty, but hope does not provide
We wonder what's around the bend, what nature will contrive

In winter's light, the senses bright, where nature hides its head
The land stripped bare, and views unscathed, reveal an open face
But features such as frost and snow, refuse to take their place
And flowers, buds and birds confused, to know their time to grace

Though seasons come, and seasons go, the World will still decide
What Man can do, and Man can take, and still exist, survive
But time will tell, as always has, and time will be the judge
If nature can, and nature will, endure the will of Man
If nature can, and nature will, endure the will of Man

Tony Langford

Intersection

Field boundaries meet at an intersection
To the north, a ragged hedge wends its way down towards the sea
To the west, an ancient path meanders invitingly at an elevated level
Sea views spill out in magnificent panorama to the distance

In this secluded corner a Hawthorn tree
Sculpted by sea breezes, bent double, arching away
Branches reach like fingers against prevailing winds
And held deep within its recesses, a midden
Capturing for posterity a collection of artefacts

Fragments of brick, flint, rolled twine, a desiccated tyre
The torn base of a bottle, letters IPSW point to a Suffolk brewery
A complete Morgan's beer bottle
Heavy and robust, in beautiful luminescent olive green

Fragments of farm implements
Heavy with rust and speaking of age
The name of Ransome, local firm, still stands out proudly
Remnants of ploughshare or threshing machine perhaps

A scene unfolds in imagination
Labourers sheltering from the noon day sun
Meagre rations and beer provide welcome respite
Encouragement for the tasks in waiting

Each item helps paint a picture, a landscape brought back to life
This is a plein air museum
Protected by encroaching undergrowth from exploring eyes
Presenting a fitting testament to the working soil
The hands of labourers, their toil and the embedded history

Tony Langford

I Hear Noises

I hear noises all around me
Chirrup do chirrup do
Sounds of birds and of grasshoppers
Chirrup do chirrup do

Sounds of reedbeds, swaying sideways
Chirrup do chirrup do
Sounds of gravel neath my footsteps
Chirrup do chirrup do

Sounds of raindrops on my jacket
Chirrup do chirrup do
Sounds of rapeseed brushing on me
Chirrup do chirrup do

Sounds of barley heads a cracking
Chirrup do chirrup do
And the tell-tale cry of curlew
Chirrup do chirrup do

Sounds of crashing waves before me
Chirrup do chirrup do
And of common terns above me
Chirrup do chirrup do

I hear noises all around me
Chirrup do chirrup do
It's the sounds of nature calling
Chirrup do chirrup do

Peter Lloyd

Lost and Found in Nature

Spine of Path

Rib of Boat

Neck of Land

Brow of Hill

Arm of Sea

Leg of Walk

Foot of Dyke

Head of Wind

Ear of Corn

Mouth of River

Eye of Storm

Shoulder of Blame

Finger of Doom

End of Days

Peter Lloyd

The Mystery of the Sea

The sea broils, fermenting and frothed

Waves forming, pushing and pulling

No pattern or shape

No direction or rhythm

No rising swell or regular flow

Just broiling, fermenting and frothed

The sea churns, muddied and brown

Peaks forming, rising and falling

No sense of direction

No movement or purpose

No sense of the tide rising at all

Just swirling, churning and brown

The sea shifts, sifting and shaping

Waves breaking, shaping the shore

Smoothing and sibilant, shaping the shore

Waves breaking, and sifting the stone

Smoothing and sibilant, shaping the shore

All shifting and sifting, sibilant sea

Peter Lloyd

Robin's wreck on Blakeney Point: (WH272)

I was the captain of this ship
When we sailed with the fleet
On a running tide out into Portland Bay
Rounding the point at Portland Bill
Hitting the tide and great Atlantic swell
My crew and I

Yet before a net was cast we fled from a storm
That blew up the Channel and scattered the fleet
Blown beyond our home port
Past Poole and Isle of Wight into waters afar
The rudder went first and then the screw
Helpless past Dover, driven on

Rescued at last we were towed away
A shambles, a mess, and a wreck
Abandoned aground
On a grey gravel spit
With our bows pointed South
A nod to our past halcyon days by Chesil Beach

(NB : WH is a Weymouth registration)

Peter Lloyd

By the Glaven

In the voice of a banded agrion:

>I flutter on banded wings
>Flapping, fragile
>
>My path unsure
>My course unsteady
>
>My second life this
>Short, bright
>
>Determined to become an ancestor
>Though never the chance to be a parent

In the voice of the river:

>I fostered you in that former life
>I sheltered you amongst the water life
>Gave succour to the nymphs
>And policed the predators
>That you might take wing
>
>Adieu
>Farewell
>Bonne chance
>Mademoiselle

Peter Lloyd

Layers of Sound: On a winter walk to Blakeney Marshes

Basso Continuo of the sea pounding
Distant noise on the shingle bank
Relentless foundation of Baroque orchestration
And Bachian walking bass chord roots

Unstructured chorus of unending sound
Random, continuous, following on
Free counterpoint of birdsong
Rustling reeds and whispering weeds

Cadenza of calls borne on the wind
Inimitable curlew's plaintive clarinet
Flighty skylark syruping higher
Pirriping pipits fluting their calls

Wailing of oystercatcher
Faint shriek of redshank and knot on the wing
All underpinned by the brassy coarse geese
And the layer of sound from the grey shingle bank

Lesley Mason

Marsh Whispers

Where silver shimmers in feathered
light, and the earth fails to follow
egrets into flight, the marsh whispers:

*Sit awhile and let me sift
your thoughts through reeds,
and stipple them with Autumn.*

*Ponder the ribbon of dark water
that meanders between the
choke of algae's vibrant green,*

*and carries the memory
of moorhen, or teal.*

*Allow the sky to settle around
your shoulders, dip-dyed blue
fading to grey where its hems
brush the land and drop
into the sea.*

Look to your feet

*and see among the leaves
that single fallen star,
a water droplet
caught on gossamer
calling down the moon.*

Lesley Mason

Back to Walsey Hills

Let's walk again along the lane
where the blackthorn grows,
over the fields where the clouds
creep low, and in the hedgerows
strange tales unfold.

Let's stand again by the four-field tree
where someone thought to plant
a ploughshare as if the Faerie would
take to farming and all the fields be
furrowed by the morn.

And someone else stashed bottles
just in case one day, beer would flow
directly from the corn.

Tell me again about the lichen shields,
that swathe the winter trees to keep them
warm and safe through the darkness where
evil spirits roam.

We'll venture again to the deep black water
where Lucifer slid down and the one
white feather spoke of his redemption,
or you can tell that sadder story, where
the last white swan did drown.

Let's clamber up the rise to watch
the sea curve round to meet the sky,
and if we can remember words and tune
share again that secret lullaby that
soothes us with the myth we choose
to live inside

that the places we hold sacred, even
as we spin our daft delights, will
somehow last forever...

and that once upon a time, will never

become that one last time.

Lesley Mason

Oak

If I sit quietly here, will you tell me a story?
I promise to be silent.

Your limbs resting on the earth, propping up
your aged trunk, less necessary without
summer's weighty crown,
provide a bench, a lap, an invitation...

Speak to me of what you know,
of the seasons you have seen,
of the games you played in your acorn days,
your sapling courtship hidden in the woods.

Teach me how to put down roots,
to hold my centre through the storms,
not to bend, but rather to not mind
being broken.

Show me how to let things go, let last year's
leaves blow away. And how to catch the
low gold of Autumn in those still green.

We're told we should grow straight and true
but your beauty is in your twisted arms
and legs, spider-sculpted. If I sit here long enough
will you unfurl, and stand up and walk away?

Or, if I stop asking questions and sit in silence with you,
will you let me stay?

Lesley Mason

Blow-ins

A skein across the storm-cleared sky,
loose-knit scouting and laying claim
to the winter grounds, they bawl
their presence, the haunting
homecoming call of geese.
These are the first to arrive,
or the last to leave, who delayed
so long they simply stayed
a whole Summer long,
not knowing they were refugees.
I flew in on an Autumn wind
pretending I'd be gone again
by season's end, but landing
in the half-tamed wild of
salty marsh and shingle,
of grey-leaved poppies
and tall feathered reeds,
where the wind steals
thoughts and throws
them to the sea…
somehow, I forgot to leave.

Maddie McMahon

Wood Woman

I am waiting woman woods,
Mulching, drinking, pausing woods,
Fertile, female, fruitful flood,
Berries scatter scarlet blood.

I am juicy, dripping woods,
Fecund, glossy, wet woods,
My roots dig deep, my branches weep,
My still, dark waters running deep.

I am wild, weaving womb woods,
Gestating, spinning Spring woods,
Burning, unfurling, naked sleeping,
Swelling, heaving, new life creeping.

I am ancient woman woods,
Wrinkled, veiny crone woods,
Mossy feet and white birch bones,
Pocked and pitted, cold as stone.

I am frigid winter woods,
Weaving wreaths for solstice woods,
Holly and Ivy shine in the night,
Writhing, entwining, seeking the light.

Maddie McMahon

Fallen Leaf

She is brown and age-spotted,
Mummified, ossified, desiccated.
Sapless veins no longer pulse
In time to the quickening bud.
She is cracked and brittle, they say,
Used and no longer of use,
Supple spring green a memory.
Fallen woman, downtrodden,
Crumbling into the sodden mulch,
Her sage words buried or slighted,
She is abandoned, branded absurd.
The view from the top given all merit,
The wisdom of the fall, unheeded.
Take a leaf out of my book
And regard her, before she is gone.

Maddie McMahon

Renaissance

Forged in amniotic ocean,
Salty womb-waters carry a current
And briny hearts begin to beat.
Born through blood, with tangy taste of sea,
Seek the ozone-aroma of areola.

Born and raised in water;
Each immersion a giving of the light*;
A labour, a courageous conquering,
A birthing of trust and faith,
A swimming in the now.

And most of all, it is the breath.
The slow, deliberate in and out.
Breathe the way in, and through;
A nativity navigation, a lachrymose labyrinth,
From heat to cold and back.

Each swim a backwards birth.
A plunge from heaviness to light,
Home, to the savoury taste of mother.
After so long, I race to be reunited,
To immerse and salinate myself.

New to the shore, the toe-dipper
Still feels the tidal tug.
Aquatic apes, we yearn for home,
Feeling the pull of the moon.
And so they hold my hand...

Stepping tentatively, in trepidation,
Shuddering and shivering,
I murmur, 'it's all in the breath'
And smile and say, 'just believe,
Because today the sea invites you.'

We slowly slip from the liminal
To liquid laughter, to revel in the joy,
To realise we have entered
The mythical place of mermaid tales
And selkie-seeking stories.

When time for landlubber legs again,
We begin the journey home.
I tell my new-born friend
That she takes the sea home on her lips,
Adds her tears to the sum of the salt.

And I remind her:
Never turn your back on the ocean,
Never turn your back on the ocean.

Dar a luz - to give light - is the Spanish term for birth

Maddie McMahon

The Sun Comes Out Eventually
After Kurt Jackson

Daybreak shingle-sitting,
Flint-crouching, solitary sentinel,
Morning tea-sipping,
Patiently breath-holding,
Awaiting dawn's first fingers
To sea-scatter silver coins.

Silent genuflection, beach benediction,
Wavelets languid-lapping,
Grey-blue blear, water-air blur,
The merest hint of fresh fire:
Horizon-pyre, pearly ocean-pavement:
Burnished pebbles, dawn-warming.

Watching newborn sky-light
And geese, like inky letters,
Winging over blotting paper,
Celestial-writing, dawn-soaring,
Barnacle-birds slipstream-surfing,
The Migration-mirage, kindred brood.

Goose guests call in the day,
Honk their promise to keep formation.
Aerodynamic collaboration,
Fowl family, imprint-bonding,
Overhead freely fluttering,
Overheard: woman wailing.

Sharon Nightingale

My North Sea

As I arrive at the shingle bank a patch of rainbow appears far to the west. I race up the bank to snatch a photo of this flash of colour in an otherwise dull sky. It doesn't fade, instead it stretches to a full arc across the sea. Incongruous in this place of muted colours, I want to ignore this show that nature is putting on for me. This is not my North Sea, the bright colours are too garish. A monochrome grey sea has been my sanctuary. It has held and soothed me. Its simplicity has calmed me. Sky, sea and beach.

> On the edge.
> As I have been too.

Lumbering, ash-coloured clouds drift across the sky to the north, reluctant to pass until they have deposited their cargo of drenching rain. It's late autumn, just a few weeks before the winter solstice, but to the south a band of azure sky recalls the scents and sounds of an English seaside in July. At sea white-shafted turbines like the masts of ships, are revealed in turn as the shifting skies drift by, each held for only a few seconds in a celestial glow. Then they merge again with the greys of a winter sky.

I need to walk, to let my mind wander. To collect my thoughts. To try and set them in some kind of order. As for so many people, life has been challenging over the last few years.

> It has fractured.
> And needs rebuilding.

Ageing raises questions too. About this life. About what is important. About where I belong.
And what I want to change before it's too late.

But I can't think. The rainbow colours are hard to ignore. A distraction. I turn and face east where I can no longer see them, this is my North Sea. I am drawn to the edge, where water meets land, by the relentless repetitive sound of the waves as they climb the shingle and then return to the sea dragging the stones back down into the depths. I breathe in deeply, but when I turn back to face land it is not just the rainbow that unsettles me. There are now too many people here, it feels too crowded. I cannot find the serenity I need. I will come back later.

*

When I return it is mid-afternoon, the rainbow has disappeared and only a few people are visible in the distance, walking the coast path. The sea has begun to encroach further up the beach, my earlier footsteps have been taken by the waves. I inhale the cold sea air and walk eastwards.

The tide has turned.
Waves pummel the land.
A roar of anger as they assault the pebbles. Rolling shingle and then… listen… a gentle hushed whisper over sand. Suddenly, a gusting, moaning, Siberian wind. My head bowed against it, the sounds reverberate inside the hood of my coat, tightened to hold a double thickness woolly hat in place. Still the waves come. Mesmerising, and relentless. In a place I am learning to call home. A fluid, shifting place that I hope can still somehow scaffold my future.

I read somewhere that we have the same percentage of salt in our blood as is in the sea. I want to believe this. I feel I am of the sea, and I wonder if there is some inherited love of the sea. Do we have a sea memory handed down in our DNA? I think we do. Most of my ancestors lived by the sea for generations. Hard lives as farmers or miners. But maybe they still loved the sea.
And maybe it is in my genes.

Then a bolt from the blue. A memory forgotten for at least fifty years. A small child, I am standing on the pebbles of a different beach, looking across a vast dark, wet plain at the sea in the distance. Warm in my memory, I can almost feel the sun on my face despite the freezing, northerly, November wind. In my mind's eye the gulls are reeling in the blue above and I can smell the delicious scent of salt on the breeze. I feel the sudden embrace of strong arms sweeping me up into the air, wrapping me in their comforting familiarity. Shivering with anticipation I am carried across the sand towards the sea. He is laughing at my fear and teasing me too, but he still takes me safely to the water's edge. My larger-than-life uncle who was my hero had saved me from the terrors of the sand, for I was scared of the worm casts that littered the sand all the way to the sea. I wonder what triggered that memory. It is my earliest memory of the sea.

A gull screeches and I realise no sand is visible now. Darkness is beginning to creep across this flat, liminal space. The sun is dropping lower, and the wind whips my face, a reminder of the power it frequently unleashes on this shapeshifting, changing landscape.

In the gloom, the sky appears lifeless at first glance, but then dark specks reveal themselves as wheeling birds in flight. A ribbon of geese career across the sky, shapeshifting as they beat against the wind; another flock follows on, then another, each competing to create the most mesmerising sculptural form. How do they know who goes where, who is leader, who is follower, is it some ancient skill passed down in their genes? The dots grow larger and reveal their heavy bodied shape, wings extended, flapping madly to stay in contention to be leader. I watch a pair of gulls wheeling in the now chrome sky before they fly over me towards the marsh behind, just over the shingle bank. One day the sea will breach this bank. Flooded, the marsh will change. And so will the beach I love. But maybe the birds will adapt.

I hope I will too.

The edges will move but they will still be there.
Edges of land and sea, that still change and merge, blurred by the tide.

Waves crash against the shingle ridge, relentless, incessant, repeating... over and over, building, rolling, crashing, renewing, refreshing and cleansing. The water-coloured sky is changing, its pale blues and greys, its lemons and whites begin to warm to shades of pink and peach, to lilac and lavender. Invisible now behind the low hills to the west, the sun is leaving its final mark on the day. Gulls skim the surface, their shadows carbon copies. A small flock gathers, descends towards the waves and then disappears into the furrows.

The noise of the waves fades as I begin to clamber up the shingle bank, pebbles slide under my feet, I am now alone on the beach. With just my thoughts. Two seals, merely metres from me, lift their heads, stare, and dip below the waves. Waves which continue to break against the shingle shelf, and I wonder how long before they breach it. Another minute, and the first one breaches the barricade, a finger of white creeps up the beach only to retreat as if burnt by the relative warmth of the stones.

The wind is biting my fingers. I spy a straggle of seaweed, the tendrils wine- coloured and papery, and next to it the stripped spine of a gull's feather laying desolate in the gloom. I pick up the bare quill and put it in my pocket. Across the marshes glows of yellow light begin to appear in the houses that are strung along the main road, and a break in the clouds causes the marshes themselves to sparkle silver as the daylight ebbs away. Above the sea, as the last few splinters of day disappear, the smoky clouds hang heavy turning the water to the darkest granite.

The first star is pricking the sky, and the noise of the wind grows louder as I drift away from the crashing and rumbling waves and then, unbelievably, as I approach the car park I spy the unmistakable outline of a barn owl.

Bewitching.
It's gliding. Beautiful in shades of white and caramel, the dusk and the lights making it glow as it swoops and whorls. It's hovering now above the marsh, above the reeds and the grasses and, astonishingly, it is letting me watch. I am transfixed, my first ghost owl. Finally, it wheels away from me and I am left standing in the car park, alone.

Barb Shannon

Blue Light

Sometimes I forget
underneath the weight of clouds
blue light is scattered like seeds
through our sky

On grey days I yearn
to be 'blue lighted'

Sometimes I remember
all I hold dear... beautiful even
is merely a trick
of light

Sometimes it is reflected
light I long for
a piercing white light
in plain sight

Cley Marshes
All Souls, 2 November 2021

Barb Shannon

Summer Solstice Walks

the Summer Solstice walks at an easy pace
she turns aside when the day is long
to look into the lemony twilight of Mouse Ear
into sun-gold yellow of Ragwort
to count black stripes on the back of the Cinnabar Moth

the Summer Solstice has time to listen
to tiny bells of pink and green ringing
to Yellow Rattle gently rasping
to whispering grasses confide in the wind
she even hears bees sip

the Summer Solstice has time...
time to lean over a wall
time to linger
to breathe deep

the Summer Solstice
has a light touch
she knows the light will lift and die
the earth will sing and sigh
She is enchantment
and wakefulness...

Wildflower Meadow Walk, Edgefield, Norfolk, 21st June 2021

Barb Shannon

RAW – Field Notes

WITNESS these lonely fields
their mono-cultured life,
our poisoned lands.
Angry rains already beat
the crops dry leave ravaged
spaces, empty places

> Still we come delighted
> with struggling scraps
> pushed to the margins
> in trampled muddied corners
> like children starved of affection
> welcoming an unkind slap

>> Our brief romance in naming parts
>> desperate to remember, colours
>> singing still into broken hearts
>> whilst we, having
>> all but forgotten them,
>> forget who we are

>>> Down on the marsh
>>> they know. Funereal wreaths
>>> For Sale and in the sky
>>> dark smudges like scars on
>>> lungs or lines rubbed out
>>> like mistakes

Visit to Four Fields, Cley-next-the-Sea, 10th August 2021

Barb Shannon

Harvest

I can just hear the field...
like bones cracking
...like light rain

I lean to listen in...
maybe it is raining
at its core?

A tiny winged insect runs across
my shadowed page

I can just hear the field
breaking at its heart...

or is it my centre
splitting apart?

Field Visit, 10 August 2021

Barb Shannon

Becoming plant-life

warm Summer morning   mid-July
sun stroking the back of my neck
rooted to the edge of the sandy hoggin path
   ...I become plant-life

hogweed, reed, grass, bindweed, sweet smelling thistle
...we weep, lean, stand tall   strong in shared space
we are umbelliferous
holding a dozen diamonds
each carrying   a score of tiny flowers   a human heart
rose pink petals outside   creamy in the middle
every miniature flower upheld on
small outward splaying green stem
we are all aloft and dreamy   floating
on our stout ridged hairy fern green legs

with us orange-red bugs with black tipped wings,
ladybugs, hoverflies in black and orange striped
strip, black-fly and tiny beetles busy
in fragrant petals   nose inside

between us suspended seed cobwebs
each reaching out to another
tiny pale brown grains each given wind assisted tentacles
fine silken threads outstretched like migrants adrift
hoping for a good wind to carry them to a new home
hoping to become plant-life
free to roam on the wind
free to settle
where they land

   Hoggin Path, Cley Marshes, July 2021

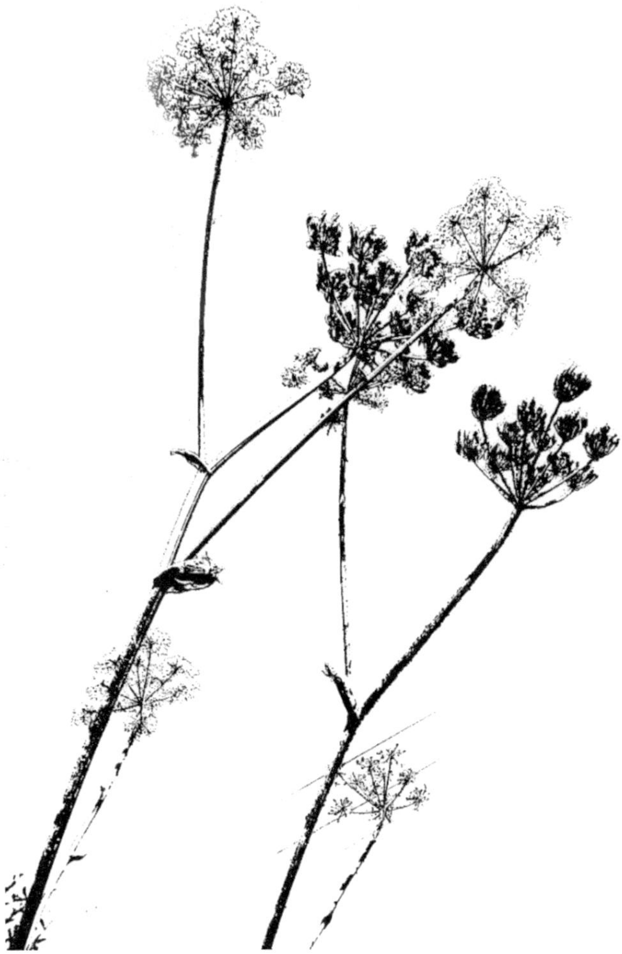

Barbara Stackwood

This is the sea – Today
17th August 2021 @noon (approx.)

Raging surf today
Crashing close and thunderous
Stones applaud
The dynamic dance of the sea
Orchestrated by the
Rhythm of the waves
The elements are glorious
Proving their power and dominance
On our existence
We need to exist with them
Recognise their worth
I feel small beside the ocean
My sense of awe and wonder is sharpened
Amazed at the feeling of isolation, although
The group of like-minded people are near
We gather to share our thoughts

Barbara Stackwood

27th July 2021

I found a fossilised sea urchin immortalised in stone. Its entity is something different now – heavy and solid, grey and defined, smooth and stable, mobility removed by the forces of nature and time, weighted down by its transition, a treasure of a long-lost soul.

Sea Urchin

Once fragile
And alive
Conceived
To survive
Now heavy
In the sand
Stone smooth
Solid in my hand
A shared find
Our favourite beach
A shared love
Now out of reach
Nature's force
Takes its toll
Now He has taken
My love's soul
That's all.

Barbara Stackwood

Immersed in Cley – 20th July 2021

Steps along a new path
Cradled by glorious grass
Drawn into the detail
Created by the history
Of this place.
Sense of souls departed
Wrapped in peace
In the layers
Of the past,
Awe and wonder
Engulf the mind.
A deception of purple
Whispering enticements
Will absorb you into
Its deadly beauty
Breathing in the clarity
Of our perceptions
Our focused awareness
And curious interest
Slows our gentle pace
As we meditate
Across this landscape
Until we reach the edge
The depths of submersion
The sea

Barbara Stackwood

Steps in Cley – 27th July 2021

Leaving population
Finding awe and wonder
Respect and admiration
Unassuming butterfly
Velvet bee
Graceful grass

I wander with my eyes
My feet follow
To that definitive edge
Of land and sea
An alien eye
Demands my attention
With its stony gaze
Seaweed is stranded
And held by its anchor
Amongst today's arrangement
Of pebbles

The gentle lullaby
Of the sea
Brings peace
And completeness
As we are embraced
In a misty haze
That limits our sight
But not our vision

Leaving the Flatland

A natural portal
Entices us into the
Blackthorn tunnel
Cradling us in
Its natural caress
It doesn't demand
Attention
Or interference.
Dank earthy tang
Hangs in the air,
Emerging into the
Light of the world.
Beyond the tunnel
The openness
Reminds us of the
Diversity we are
Privilege to.
Scratchy fingers
Keep us on the narrow path.
Soporific poppies
Embrace their treasure
Secretly
Should we lie here
Perchance to dream

Chris Tassell

Glandford Glimmers
A quartet of 5-minute experiences.
November 9th, 2021. Sunny 12c. Brisk S/W breeze.

One: "Pebbles in the ford"
Where the river ripples shallow up to the dry dipping road
Loose pebbles take on two different lives.
Dry — they are a dull lot, mostly shades of grey.
But where the river pushes glassy wet fingers forward
They become as bright jewels set in aspic.
When the breeze catches and plays with the surface
All blurs to a dream river of renewed expectations.

Two: "Tree stumps by the stream"
Four small poplars felled at useful heights are lecterns for notebooks.
Scrubby willows drop yellow fish to join silver minnows whilst the
River hurries, hurries — always white rabbit late.
A heron scolds and church bells haul our dreaming to present time.

Three: "Wind in the poplar"
The poplar whispers softly to the river: "Why do you rush?
Stay awhile and I will tell you what I see.
Distant slopes and brooding woods where a buzzard mews.
Listen to my ancient songs. Slow you down, the sea will wait."

Four: "Seated on a log in the meadow."
One end of this log is dryly and wetly rotting with worm and beetle
Crumble. Finger loose it falls to feed the grateful grass.
At the other end life is reasserting itself with new stems
Half-a-yard high, soon to be a thicket for birds.

Chris Tassell

A Brief Encounter at Bayfield Woods
November 8th, 2022. 13°C Light S\W breeze. Mainly sunny.

We are gathered on a fallen rowan tree
  For reading and writing, disturbing woodlouse city.
  These miniature armadillos thrive under the parchment bark.

As I sit, a drowsy wasp lands on my knee — without leave.
  The sort of wasp that in the fading Summer
  Ravaged my beautiful apples leaving only paper skins.

That frenzy over, it means no harm and feels safe here.
  It starts to clean its feelers with delicate front legs,
  Much as I wipe my glasses for a better view.

Cleaning done, the wasp enjoys warm fabric below,
  And the late Autumn sunshine filtering through the trees.
  Anxious not to disturb its reverie I speak to it gently:

"Now you are rested what is your plan
  Because I need to move my leg?"
  With a slightly waspish edge it replied:

"If you are bored with my company I will return to the
  Hedge where the crabs are rotting sweetly,
  And then to the village to find a shed for Wintering."

  And off it buzzed murmuring, "Thanks for the apples."

Chris Tassell

Cley East Beach on the dunes
October 21st, 2021. Very strong South-Westerly. Warm 20°C. Cloudy.

"Stirred by a bird"

Sea to my back, notebook in hand, I am distracted
By a bird which joined us to show how to master the wind
Stealing words from the page before they could arrive.

It was a wind cuffer, a wind bibber, a wind fanner,
A wind hover, which we call a kestrel.
A bird by any name could not possess more skill.

Its control of the strong breeze was a wonder to behold.
Head into wind, held still by wings and tail, the ballet continued
With sudden plunges controlled by smooth puppetry.

Did it possess some basic instinct to be near man?
To be near those who admire such birds.
In the courts of the world, eagles for a king, kestrels for a knave.

Once, it showed us its falcon's stoop.
Wings held rigidly aloft, spilling the useful air. Claws grasping
It left the buoyant wind to fall on a plumb-line.

It missed the vole and whilst on the ground we talked.
I asked, "Why do you leave your homely woods and hedgerows
To seek prey at the salty, rough sea edge?"

It looked at me with a disdainful eye
Which just said, "Tasty saltmarsh lambkin pie!"

Chris Tassell

Cley East Beach
August 8th, 2023. Sunny, 15°C. N/W breeze.
"To be with the sea for 30 minutes"

I settle on the strand and immerse my thoughts
Just beyond the creamy fingers of the tide
Which tries to wet my feet for fun.

A Canute moment occurs to me. I know the turn is due.
I looked it up. I know the sea's next move.
So why didn't he check his tide table?

Mesmerized by the rhythm of breaking water
I want to press pause just as the wave's lip turns over
To explore that sun-lit moment which we never see.

This movement is so relentless and restless it lulls the brain
To listen deeply to the sounds it creates.
Waves crash, splash and pebbles grind with noisy complaint.

Sea music comes to me — Debussy — Britten — Wagner.
A 1950s radio sings "La Mer" by a handsome Frenchman
Housewives' delight. "Voyez les oiseaux blancs."

Our birds today are a squabble of terns.
They catch the sun in a flash of delight.
The sea has seen it all before and carries on with its day.

Chris Tassell

Coastwise
Blakeney Quay. February 11th, 2020. Sunny, very windy.
"Blow winds and crack your cheeks!" * *Read with feeling.*

YOU Breath stealer, eye stinger, toothacher, finger tingler.
YOU Branch-snapper, tree feller, tile crasher, beach hut smasher.
YOU Wavecrestskimmer, spume maker, tide pusher, storm creator.
YOU Sailsplitter, sheet slapper, spinnaker filler, yacht de-master.
YOU Buzzardsoarer, kestrel hoverer, red-kite tail twister.
YOU Leafherder, jetsam piler, cloud chaser, light changer.
YOU 50mph guster, bridge closer, lorry turner, umbrella insideouter.
YOU Powerlinesparker, meal spoiler, sleep stopper, fencedowner.
WE Fear you coming, YOU whining trouble maker.
NOW GO! BE calmer. YOU cobweb clearer. YOU mind refresher.

Cley Beach. July 26th, 2022. Light breeze from North.

The sea was waiting for us,
Waiting to be written about — feeling important.
Flexing its muscles, flinging pebbles about in an arrogant fashion.
Demanding attention, filling the horizon — declaring its omnipotence.

We call it the North Sea, but it encircles our planet in many guises —
Oceans, seas, channels, bays, gulfs, straits, passages, firths, fiords, lochs.
But what's in a name? They are all part of the same joined wetness.
Terrifying, useful, and never tamed — but great — for swimming in.

* from *King Lear,* William Shakespeare

Heather Tyrrell

At The Summer Solstice

WINDBLOWN memories

    BLUR on a

        SMUDGED-EQUINOX June morning

        Of cool **STILLNESS**

        And **CONSTANT** joy

    Surrounded by **DANCING** grasses

In mist-smeared **LIGHT**

    Veiling **CHAOTIC**

        Global **MIGRATION**

        A world **PIVOTING** in heat

Fewer swifts

This is an uncoiled version of the book's Frontispiece.
*The words in **bold** were chosen by individual members of a writing group at the end of a walk on Cley beach, North Norfolk. **Constant** was my word of the morning.*

Heather Tyrrell

"If we don't act now, it will be too late."
Sir David Attenborough 2022

I won't be quiet!

I will feel quiet *once*
vehicle engines hush their noise
visitors stop asking for directions
walkers don't apologise for getting in my way
the droning paraglider disappears

I will feel calmer once I *can*
    find those wigeon whistling way off left
identify that flock of gliding, weaving, circling birds
ignore the criss-crossing vapour trails
feel this raw landscape filling my nostrils, my ears and eyes, my inner self

I will feel quieter *once*
the steady plod of footsteps travel this track
    'Radio Wild' rides the airwaves
    a chance to slow the heart rate
    and hear nature breathing, living, getting by

I will be quiet *when*
    threats of rising global tides subside
    wind turbines, far out at sea, power every home
flocks of lapwings truly fill the skies in their thousands upon thousands like a century ago

I can't be calm, and I won't be quiet
    a stiffening breeze steals this chance of contemplation
    blows harder, reminds me, challenges me
    not to become complacent or accept false promises
    in the days ahead
    stand firm it calls, prepare to act
    pick up that banner
    and roar

        ENOUGH! ENOUGH! ENOUGH!

Heather Tyrrell

Retrospective

An avocet in shallow waters

A lapwing nestled on eggs

A pair of snowy owls

A barn owl on silent wing.

Skyscape of flying swans, white on white

Cormorants and spoonbills at sunset

Flightless blackbirds on colourful stamps

A grey heron adorns a rectangular table mat.

Birds wading, fishing, preening

Soaring, roosting, motionless

Alert, alive,

Calling.

Avian life in lino and inks

Transposed from a Norfolk landscape

To the lens-like hands of a master printer

That was Robert Gillmor.

Inspired by a retrospective exhibition of Gillmor's works at the Cley NWT Visitor Centre.

Ann Haley Wade

Cormorant

It was summer, bold August afternoon
that I saw it lie on the tide-thrown strand
spread out like the Cross.
A cloak of dazzled feathers, such sun-drenched
black, such invitation.
Oh my! I put it on at once,
assumed dark plumes. Slipped off my soul
as I would my wedding ring, with oil.

The cloak was light but I was not.
With greed I could not soar but plunged
beneath the waves: a fishing-spear
sinking my bill and hook,
un-fearing all but the curse of Fisher Kings offshore,
their wires and lines casting me off.

Ann Haley Wade

Miranda by the Sea

"O Wonder!
How many godly creatures are there here!
How beauteous mankind is! O
brave new world that has such people in't."
      from *The Tempest,* William Shakespeare

my daughter
out from the waves you crowned yourself
with seaweed, glutinous fronds dripped from your arms
shells and sea-glass enrapt

you were Nereid at the tide's edge
siren to glee

my daughter
it seems a storm is coming, in a thousand years
they said,
tempest, drought and flood
in a hundred years, wildfires out of control

now they speak
a lifetime's span, Earth turning to silence

my daughter
do not say extinction

when you swam inside me, for the first time
future became present, my dreams
promises that may not be kept

my daughter, do not say hopeless
to the sky and the trees
to the waterfalls

to all life-bearing things

my daughter
when you swim in the sea

Ann Haley Wade

Old Path in Spring

find your own way, you said, as those before you have done

bracken foxglove birch

bumblebee buzzing its low-ground hum

slope dry moth

sandy bank covered by chiffchaff song

lichen mosses root

path once taken, softly slipping among

frond bark den

in old age, what's been felled, wants to grow again

opening unfurl stump

Ann Haley Wade

Mother Courage in Salthouse *

How many times she crossed she could not say,
it was man's folly put a *Rocket* on the Eye, to build
Hell under a church.
Still she pulled samphire & salt crust from mud,
knew the art of preservation,
a true artist in the art of living low.
Daughter of the Late Valiant he gets all the
adjectives, left nothing attached to her, though
before she died surely *She* lived was not without
Quality.
From a long *Dew* line stretched out as far as the eye
could not see, over Salthouse shingle banks, endless
heaving and repairing. She owned a brigantine,
held sway but was never *Captain*.
And in the great *Rage* when tide turned full in the
eye of the wind, upped the sails of her skirts, laid
hold of a precious thing or two – her children.

She had nothing, not the *Common Right* but the
common sensing of the sea uprising twenty
minutes before engulfment.
Alone at last the wife of *Someone* very important,
a lone woman guarding her solitude,
surrounded only where sea broke
stones, she was happily defenceless,
such fun I won't let you spoil my war.
'Till the boys rowed out to get her.
It was men's folly made shelter on the hill
for the dead. For the living, *Sea Level*.

* See Appendix for footnotes to this poem

Bob Ward

Dragonflies

Three hundred million years
   they've hung around, hawking
   over ponds, the senior predators
   ever assured in what they do.

While nymphs they had emerged
   as underwater terrorists,
   lurking hidden among reeds
   for some tadpole to stray close,
   when hinged jaws would act,
   spring out, strike with precision.

Eventually they scaled tall stems
   to throw off their drab armour
   and reappear in technicolour,
   become the vibrant glitterati,
   dashing masters of the air.

Hovering, they will square up to you,
   viewing you as the mere creature
   that you might happen to be.

If you try to match their gaze,
        eye to eye, they never blink.

Bob Ward

Saltmarsh Creek

That's where you find them,
    scarlet legs the give-away,
    redshanks briskly pattering across
    grey mud you wouldn't trust.

Beaks probe silt deeply
    to yank up squirmy gobbets
    gulped down whole before
    they could even spawn
    a verse in their own right.

The birds lurk at creek margins
    between mud and salty swill,
    constantly alert, on edge.

If disturbed, they bristle off
    with shrill indignant cries:
    "When did I ever want
    to get snared by your poem?"

But I'll make no apology,
    this time. I also stalk life's edges.

Bob Ward

Along the Way

The narrow footpath ran between reeds fringing a dyke and an overgrown roadside verge. On the ground in front of me was a tortoiseshell butterfly basking in the sunlight. I stopped to watch as it slowly closed its wings, opened them again, closed, reopened then remained still, absorbing the warmth. Stepping carefully past I managed to avoid disturbing it.

A little further on I came cross a second butterfly, this time a peacock flaunting its bright eyes. One of William Blake's *Proverbs of Hell* declared that "The pride of the peacock is the glory of God". He had the bird in mind though I expect that he would have embraced this creature as well. But any glory here was fading; the butterfly was dead beyond any chance of revival. I was able to pick it up to appreciate better the sumptuous tapestry of its wings. After replacing it on the ground I continued the walk.

What I found next proved to be different, a red-buttoned ball-point pen carelessly dropped by a stranger. It was never alive, yet I can bring life to it by writing this.

Bob Ward

Going to Seed

If you happen to be unwell, you might say that you were feeling seedy. "Why is this?" I wonder. Surely, seeds deserve better than a crude association with illness.

With the end of summer many plants die down, but they leave messages to the future in the form of seeds. Although such seeds are often small, they carry the potential of renewed life. On germination they thrust a root into nourishing soil, while a shoot reaches upwards towards the light. Think of Jack's beanstalk; climb after him.

The diverse forms that a seed may take fascinate me. They are always worth close attention, under a lens if necessary. I am thrilled to have Goat's Beard in my garden, the Big Ben among flower clocks, a masterpiece of botanical engineering. The umbels of Hogweed carry platelets, each containing a pair of slim seeds. Within each glossy globe of a Blackberry there is a pip liable to get caught between your teeth. Bulrushes line the dykes on Cley Reserve. Their seeds begin as a brown muff sleeved along a spike. Gradually the muff disintegrates into fluff bearing minute promises about the sturdy plant into which they could transform. The slender pods of Rosebay Willowherb peel apart releasing wisps of silk that float away bearing tiny seeds.

In autumn, I find that I have a special affection for the Alexanders. The plants' white shrunken stems carry bunches of black nuggets, like sculptures made from coal. But they also have a story to tell. This is not an indigenous plant. It was brought in by the Romans because they enjoyed the leaves for a salad. As the Romans made their way along the Norfolk coast, they left a trail of Alexanders, which have become a living relic of that distant invasion, requiring no archaeologists to uncover. The process of going to seed deserves attention and we need to pay it due respect. After all, our daily bread is made from seeds.

Bob Ward

Language of the Land

Listen . . . Listen . . . Listen . . .
　for the land has many voices, dialects,
　uttered by diverse agencies.
Mark how winds in conversation with the reeds
　move on provoking whispers among pines.
In darkness catch the red deer's rutting bellow,
　or the muntjac's bark just beyond your fence.
Bees buzz, squirrels scold, magpies chatter endlessly,
　grazing across Cley marsh the brent geese gossip.
Later an owl hoots down your chimney pot
　and a snorting hedgehog bundles through a bush.
In spring, note the birds in morning chorus
　competing for the season's territories.
Let yourself attend a stream tumbling around a rock
　where a dipper likes to perch and sing.
Then be surprised by the abrupt splash of a trout
　as it surfaces to snatch a passing fly.
When abroad, if climbing mountains
　hear stressed alpine glaciers groan,
　edging across a valley shelf.
Or In Iceland, stand well back from a geyser's roar
　venting super-heated steam up high,
　voicing the syntax of tectonic plates.
Mind too, the altercations that arise,
　when the precious land confronts invasive seas.
Whatever the voice, the message stays the same:
　this worn land must be cherished for all time.
And this land also needs you to speak up for it.

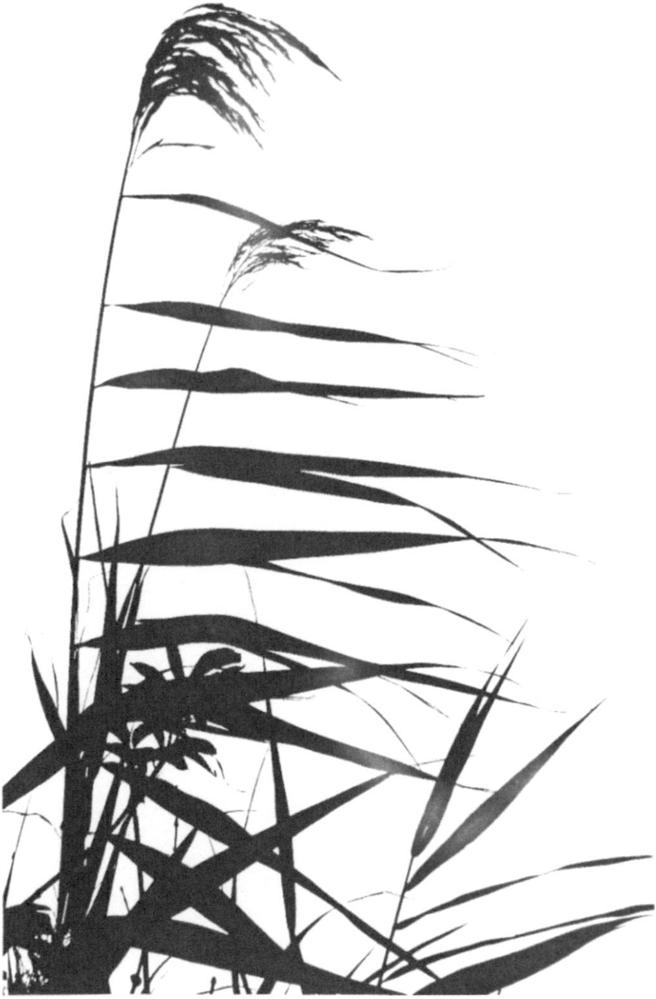

Jonathan Ward

Patience
for my father

(1)
I learnt to walk with you—

pathways, lanes, tracks,
local walks cut through

fringes of countryside,
or round by the old farm

past the poet's cottage
silent behind box hedges,

its dark windows
sometimes candlelit,

watching birds, flowers,
listening to trees,

seeing the seasons
change in the hedgerows,

learning to name, to love
small places and their ways,

owl cries at dusk
in the lane, the smell of fox,

rooks screwing out rain
from a greying sky,

the bright colours
of the butterfly bush

—to attend to small things.

(2)
Patience
to wait for the seed

to grow strong,
today ruby chard

alight in early morning
autumn sunlight

jewels of a treasure cache
from the earth.

Patience
to stand

at the entrance
to a field

watch
the clouds move,

the shifting
light,

first one
swallow

then more
come closer

displaying
white breast

red and
silhouette

the more so
the longer we are

silent
and still.

Patience
to learn

to read
the world

its gentle pulls
and plays.

Patience
when the body

fails,
its slow decay

returning to earth
and light.

Patience
to see in

the darkening field
a greater darkness

around
the edges;

and to see
the lane brighten

at a gap in the hedge
opening out

to horizons
sun breaking through

above the bracken,
illuminating.

Jonathan Ward

A Gift
Hunworth Ford, Garlic Wood

Back again from a walk
still elated at finding
a new track through woods,
across a fast-flowing ford
where we stopped to listen
to the running water
and watch a grey wagtail,
its long up and down tail like a wand.
It is a gift this place
where I have been brought by a friend
and walking up through the woods
he taught me his father's old word
netherbackwashes—
just randomly following lanes or tracks
and seeing where you end up.
Like writing.

Jane Wilkinson

Funeral ceremony for a dogfish

We come on foot, collect ourselves to cross the salt marsh,
along a rammed earth dyke, bringing to the sea whatever ails.
In the percussive reed leaves, one of us is left behind,
as an anchor against the wind, that is what we agreed.

*

When the flint falls open like an Easter egg, like dawn,
it's shared out. I kneel at the edge, with my back to the congregation
of waves and read the universe, a sermon from a blotchy page.
Undiscovered planets live on the beach, the moon, lens flare,
sulphur for incense. Was this stone once re-entry ballast?
Flint it seems – like this sea – is unsolvable.

*

Gathering above us, salt grey clouds enter each other;
rag edges emulsify. More things are brought for the altar:
the dogfish is carried on the palms of your hands
and a cuttlefish pit, its embryonic bone,
pure white mineral, like soap washed to a blade.
Then mostly plastic, a daily scripture heaped in mouthfuls.
And bladderwrack: a blister pack
of oxygen in bitter-iodine brown. I notice, however cold
and sabotaged the pie-crust crab shell is, it is still intact.
We deliberate a single oily glove: petrol blue
and four sizes too big for anyone.
More feet smash across the beach.

*

All pray for this lesser-spotted dogfish.
In praise, our words spit in the air. The small rain brings
a cormorant to preside at our midden.
Yes, feathered lines like that should take flight.

                    *

We strike the set. The committal of our crown of treasures
is capsized to a tidemark. We loot it, bag the extra-terrestrial shark.
Then stand around the burnt remains of our actions, for a moment,
go for lunch, leave our salt in the wind.

Jane Wilkinson

Down Reading Room Loke and straight on to

the grasshopper field

> common yarrow is devil's nettle, old man's pepper, soldier
> woundwort; it grows with field poppies. A clear plastic tube
> sweats with the breath of an oak sapling's first full leaves. Each
> of my steps raises a separate splash of grasshoppers; if I sit still
> they purr in stereo. I know the sea dreams under this field,

and the toad field

> past knotted hawthorn, elderflower, ivy, find barley
> baking under the thick heat, honeyed with lady's bedstraw.
> Bees sail by. From this distance tyre-black marsh cows
> gather and scatter and gather. On the dust path a toadlet,
> small as a lost jacket-button, and toadflax flowers or
> *butter-and-eggs* – as if you've only just started to cream them,

and the seagull field

> I'm way behind in this small dark wood
> between fields, cool as a larder. The field rises
> and falls like sea swell. Inside the soothing song
> of the barley hair is a godly hiding place; I don't
> want to be found. I go in and pull it over me,

and the lark field

the woods beyond this field contain their dark
moisture the way clouds do. A bedtime smell,
from the other side of the hedge, a settlement
of common camomile, a field inside
a field, with a side-field of cabbage, their meaty
leaves clap. Each species releases its own
temperature. I've nothing so good as an answer,
for the larks, or any of the field's variations,

and the helicopter field

a high field, a table field, unfolding its bright metallic cloth
to the heath green corners. Sweet percussive wheat music.
A scattering of corn marigold, coins of concentrated sunlight.
The steeple and the sea turbine, two antennae signalling
across the fields – the wheat's reply is blown away.

Jane Wilkinson

Father in a summer wood

Leaving behind the poppies at the field margin,
I was variegated in the bracken's polka-dot shade,

shook it off in the cool of a blackthorn edge
brooding for sloes. One crow flew into the field,

dissolved under the plaited wheat heads sweating
gold. I turned uphill to the heath, to a sea

of rippling copper-wire grass, rattling for wildfire,
encircled with oak woods stunted by loamy soil

and coast winds. As I lay face down in the dry moss
and rabbit droppings, to escape the sun,

vertical summer bloomed. Death by August.
A grasshopper wound down, and the mouth

of the earth spat up its loose shrapnel flints. Gorse
spiders waited in complex webs. On a worn path

through the trees, I smelt him in last year's
leaf-fall, roasting in the heat; out of its ripe tobacco

came the clicking pipe in his mouth, my father
conjured in Golden Virginia smoke and snapped twigs.

Peter Wilson

Finding a Whale

I saw a whale among the woodland carpet.
Looking again, it was a seal.

So far from the sea? I picked it up.
It did not seem to mind; I turned it over; no, a whale.

Quite small for a whale, even for a seal. And dry.
But against the sunlight it had that sea-wet darkness.

Like every sea-creature it was smooth, honed by waves,
Battered in the tides,

Nibbled by other sea-creatures and various crustacea.
Carefully I gave it a little hug to show it I loved it,

And would return it to the sea,

Drive it gently to the shore at Cley and set it free in the German Ocean.

Then I dropped it, on my foot. Ouch! It was a cobble. Ungrateful beast.

Peter Wilson

April 1992
Inspired by Wiveton Down, April 2022

There's an old stone bridge, sheep shorn grass, the ruins of last autumn's bracken subsiding back into the earth. There's a brook, moody and withdrawn today. A few tumbled stones and twisted grey branches close by show that it is not always so reticent. On the grass are light brown pellet signs of rabbits, and darker stains of sheep.

But this is not the place; this is just where we start. Half hidden by collapsing bracken is a path. It begins a winding ascent among rocks, its narrow way cut by the sharp hooves of sheep, with the occasional half-eroded boot print to prove we are not unique. The path hugs us tight and sidles up through the bracken, twisting sideways up the dale bank, onto the empty wiry blackness of the moor, always taking the easy way.

In August all this land wears a purple coat, but now, having shrugged off the late snow, the heather waits for the sun to bring life back. Up, and to the right; up, and to the left; up, along and up. Then we are on the ridge. Here the path straggles wide, the stones and thin soil slipping away to either side, patches of grass, a few outcrops of heather.

No movement. No sheep; no rabbits. Another month, there will be small birds keeping their distance, by July, adders sunbathing on the path. The rabbits are always there, somewhere. The sheep will come out from the sheltered places, drifting from grass patch to grass patch. Insects will abound, if waited for. Maybe a curlew will cry far away. The grouse are here now, those that survived last autumn's battue* and last winter's ice. No sight of them, but from not so far away come their short sharp calls, warnings to the curious.

The wind is almost still, the sky is almost clear. To the northeast, the blue shimmer of the sea, beyond pale red roofs and the cliff edge ruin of an abbey, defiant still at the very edge of the land.

But we rarely saw it. We always looked the other way, to the other horizon, twenty miles distant. There, though only to those that know it is there, was the little hilltop wood that sheltered home. My father was not much of a man for travelling. This was his idea of a perfect journey. An hour from home and check that the little wood held his sanctuary tight.

battue – the driving of game towards the hunters.

Peter Wilson

The Rabbit Bank

The autumn equinox. The season ends, the year turns. In confusion. For long the rains failed to arrive, until at last they made up for their summer modesty by a series of deluges. The formerly dry earth was already coated with the golden glow and sienna decay of approaching winter many weeks too early. But nature has her own ways, is not bound by human definitions; and now, to spite all rules and expectations, she has suddenly adopted spring-like green. The expected colours of late autumn, the falling leaves, the crushing down of nettles and bracken, the late rich red and black fruits of tree and hedgerow, were suddenly repulsed. Instead, all is pretending to be young, fecund, and emerald sharp. Flowers bloom a second time, berries reawaken and fatten, the vegetable plot resumes its generous giving, the trees lift up weakened limbs and stand proud once more. The apples, having dozed idly on spindly branches, gross up. As do the maggots feeding on them.

And on the church walk, the fields now cleared and ploughed, the rabbits, thin but with energy revived, look cautiously across the long valley and ponder the shortening of days. Their life cannot return to what it was. The rabbit bank was hacked and chopped and scythed short in the late spring. The rabbits moved away, not far, just to the other, shady, side of the field, into old burrows cleared and new ones excavated.

They have fled many times before; it is part of the cycle of life in this field, in this colony of conies. When the grass grows long again and the blackberry stems provide armour against the curious, when the elder revives and the nettles hide the burrow entrances, then they go back. But this summer the rains stayed away, the clouds, full of promise, did not deliver what seemed certain.

Nothing grew on the rabbit bank, there was no recovery, the warren stayed exposed, there was no place for young to feed; then the old entrances collapsed. The fox came often to the top of the bank and looked down.

Then, leg raised, he stared across the cornfield, until half camouflaged by the prematurely ripened barley he made his silent way across, through the thin crackling stems, in hunger and hope.

The rabbits will not return home this year. Too late for excavating their complex diggings, still too dry to risk life in the deep tunnels, too easy for the fox to dig his way in, nothing much growing on the steep, sheared slope to hide their presence from enemies all around. No easy feasting until the new spring growth comes. And nothing to conceal gentle herbivores from the increasing anger and violence and hunger of winter. They may have lived on the bank for hundreds of years but this winter they must make temporary camp elsewhere. Until, they hope, the spring equinox lets whoever survives go home, to start that old life again.

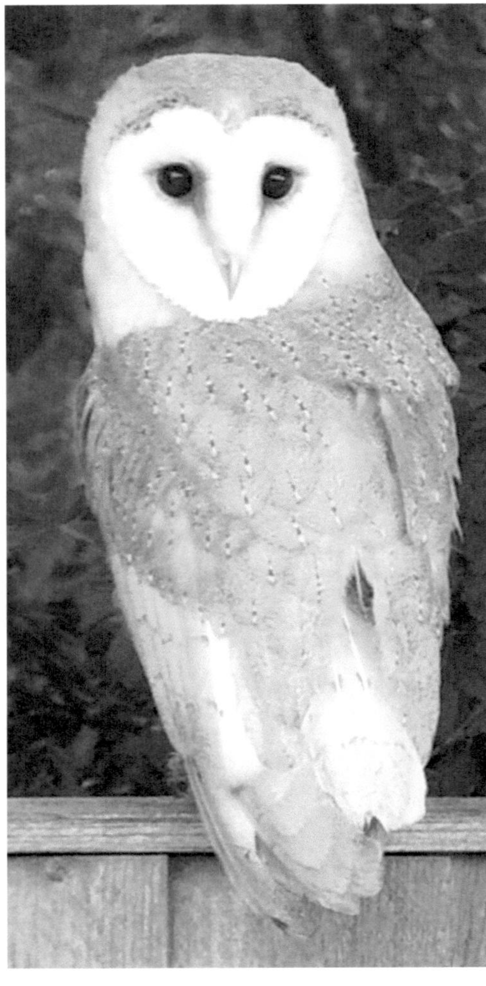

Appendix

* Footnotes for *Mother Courage in Salthouse* by Ann Haley Wade

This poem conflates (and takes liberties with) stories of some ordinary and extraordinary Salthouse women, now marvellously recorded by local historians, notably The Salthouse History Group. Words in italics are a nod to historic documents where a word or phrase considered important enough was capitalised or written in more elaborate fashion.

For sources see: www.salthousehistory.co.uk

Salthouse, The Story of a Norfolk Village, Stagg, Frank; Fiddian, Val [ed.], The Salthouse History Group, Salthouse, 2003.

Norfolk Places, Jane Hales, Boydell Press, 1975 (also in the above book). Hales tells the story of a young mother, Ruth, who rescued her children from The Great Rage, a massive storm in 1897, and 'lay hold on a thing or two'.

'Daughter of the Late Valiant', ascribed to Mary Myngs, daughter of Admiral Sir Christopher Myngs on her gravestone in St. Nicholas' Church.

Dew – in the 1860s Susanna Dew owned shares in a brigantine. *Hell* was the name given to a room beneath the church.

Common Right refers to the entitlement of some villagers – commoners – to graze animals on Salthouse Common.

Rocket – built in the mid-nineteenth century by Onesiphorus Randall, the Rocket House, also known as Randall's Folly, was destroyed in the huge flood of 1953. In WW2 an officer's wife living there was marooned after yet another flood and had to be rescued by men rowing out from the village.

Authors

Susanne Anderson spent her teenage years in North Norfolk. She draws her creative inspiration from observing the tenacity and optimism of the flora and fauna that clings to the coastline, against a rising sea and tempestuous climate. She uses natural metaphors in her work as a clinical hypnotherapist and to sustain self-resilience when life is at its most tumultuous.

Sue Boag is a lover of art and literature who finds inspiration in the everyday marvels of the world. She can often be found with her head in the clouds looking for her particular love: Birds of Prey. Born in London, she retired to Norfolk, where she discovered strong family roots going back several generations.

Jacqueline Bryony writes poetry in order to illuminate and make sense of her lived experience. She believes it is hard work being a person. She values kindness, empathy and being close to the sea as she strives to understand what it means to be a human being rather than a human doing.

Sue Burge lives in North Norfolk, close to the sea. Her poems have been widely published and have also featured in anthologies on science fiction, modern Gothic, illness, Britishness, endangered birds, WWI and the pandemic. Sue's third collection, *The Artificial Parisienne*, was published by Live Canon in January 2024.

Adam Curtis has been a Nature Reserve Manager for 35 years. His written narratives on wildlife and countryside management have been published in journals, books, and newsletters. A recent move to North Norfolk has given Adam the opportunity to be more creative in his writing.

Kathrine Drakley is a Poet/Lyricist/Photographer with a deep love and connection to the natural world that has influenced her written and photographic work.

Annie Giraud was born in a coastguard station between the North Sea and a lighthouse. She penned a few pantomimes before turning to fiction for young adults. Nowadays, the gymnastics of writing poetry outside keep her wide awake. She has read 720 Geographical Magazines over the last 60 years.

Tina Green is an aspiring writer and artist. She takes inspiration from walks through nature and the camaraderie of like-minded writers, informed by a keen scientific interest and a long career in medicine. She enjoys performing and sharing her work aloud with others.

Cornel Howells writes about wildlife and the countryside. He is a conservation volunteer and species recorder. From an upbringing in the seclusion of the New Forest to retirement under the wide skies of North Norfolk he finds scope for his other interests of weather and landscape and light.

Amanda Jane was born in Norfolk and still lives in the County. She has always been surrounded by and submerged in nature. Writing about the world around her brings her such joy and peace. Nature's ever-changing resources are plentiful for a writer like her.

Tony Langford is a Norfolk boy with a love of the countryside, particularly the Wensum valley. Relatively new to the delights of creative writing, he enjoys immensely the company and talents of teachers and fellow writers. The link between the written word, music and nature inspires much of his work.

Peter Lloyd has always dabbled in the creative arts, and during a sabbatical in 2013 wrote a blog encompassing travels across Europe, Iceland and the Arctic. On moving to Norfolk, his writing style developed to capture his love of the natural world; never happier than finding inspiration along the coast.

Lesley Mason is a poet, blogger, and gentle walker, writing from the heart, looking for beauty, sharing wisdom, trying to be kind. In 2024 she was awarded the Oberon Herbert Prize and short-listed for the Teignmouth Poetry Festival open prize. Her reflective blog and short-form poems are at www.lesleya.com

Maddie McMahon is a doula, doula trainer and breastfeeding counsellor. Author of two books about birth and motherhood. She blogs at thebirthhub.co.uk grappling with the perennial themes of birth, transition and female growth and empowerment.

Sharon Nightingale is inspired by the land, water and people of East Anglia. A collector of walks, swims and stories, she intertwines the challenges of our world with memories and the depths of human emotions. Exploring with a sense of wonder and reflection, her journeys are both fun and thought-provoking.

Barb Shannon loves the way writing outdoors can transform a simple walk into communion with life itself. Especially drawn to plant life, the minutiae and the intricate beauty of nature she writes to remember and sometimes simply to accept. She adores cats and has a tendency to wander.

Barbara Stackwood appreciates the diverse experiences to be found in the creative and performance arts. She loves being at the heart of her family. She is community spirited and believes in kindness, respect and compassion. Barbara's contribution to this anthology is a new venture for her.

Chris Tassell is a writer of poetry and prose influenced by a love of nature and the North Norfolk countryside. Writing has come late in life, inspired by Jonathan Ward's Cley sessions which he joined on day one. Writing outside has become a life-enriching experience.

Heather Tyrrell is a volunteer for the Norfolk Wildlife Trust. She writes outdoors for the sheer pleasure of being in nature and with nature. She conjures with words and ideas to convey her deep concern for the natural world, including the North Norfolk coast, but also takes time to celebrate its beauty, complexity and influence.

Ann Haley Wade is a poet. Her work is inspired by the landscape, nature, and people of East Anglia – where she has lived and worked for most of her life – and by too much reading. She works in the criminal justice system.

Bob Ward is a poet/photographer with a scientific background. North Norfolk richly sustains his long-standing fascination with wildlife. His poems embedded in photographs were exhibited at the Poetry-next-the-Sea Festival in Wells (2011). Publications include *Fortunes of the Negative* (2000); *Lines of Inquiry* (2017); *In and Out of Doors* (2023)

Jonathan Ward lives in rural North Norfolk. He began running the Writing Outside workshops at NWT Cley Marshes in spring 2016. His poems have appeared in a variety of magazines, chapbooks and exhibitions. His full-length collections are *Swallows in Late September: New and Selected Poems* and *A New Path*.

Jane Wilkinson is a writer, mother and landscape architect with a background in Fine Art. Her first collection is *'Eve Said'* (Live Canon 2023). She has won writing competitions including Live Canon Collection Prize, Aesthetica Poetry Prize and Poetry Society's Hamish Canham Prize; and is widely published in magazines and anthologies.

Peter Wilson fled the City, carrying ink, paper, and hope. And a banana. Now he writes for two on-line magazines on politics (mainly American), and gardens, pursues steam engines, and, best of all, loves the wildness, history, architecture, and beauty of North Norfolk.

Acknowledgements

The editorial team of Sue Burge, Lesley Mason, Bob Ward and Jonathan Ward have enjoyed collaborating to bring this book to the world. We are grateful for the enthusiastic support of all the contributors, and for the patience of partners and friends who have put up with our preoccupation in pulling this together.

There are a huge number of other people without whom this would not have become the book that it is, so we would also like to thank the following...

Publisher John Murray for permission to the Ronald Blythe quote from *Next to Nature* in our introduction; Harriet Tarlo for the phrase *'writing outside'* which Jonathan adopted for the Cley workshops and for her inspiration which continued to feed through them for many years; Janette Dalston of *North Norfolk Amnesty International* for coming up with the inspired phrase *"Language of the Land"* which spoke so well of what we do and her permission for us to adopt it as our title for this anthology; Barbara Stackwood for the evocative embroidery and tapestry depiction of the layers of the Cley landscape which formed the basis for our cover and Jane Wilkinson for her help with the overall cover design; Jane Wheeler for permission to include *'blackthorn tunnel'*; Heather Tyrell for her spiral solstice capture that gifted us the frontispiece; nature-and-soul-centred writer and coach Jackee Holder for permission to use her words about writing in community; Patrick Barkham for enthusiastic support and his generous foreword; and Miriam Darlington and Matt Howard for taking time to read the advance copy and their kind thoughts which appear on the rear cover of this volume.

Thanks also to all the nature writers, poets, historians, essayists, artists and storytellers (too many to list) whose published works have provided literary and pictorial inspiration, workshop ideas, and flora and fauna identification aids, all of which have helped us to understand what it is we are looking at or listening to out in the field and how to tap into our responses to that environment; to all the members of the group over many years who have generously shared their personal stories, and draft pieces and, on a more practical level, their car-space on our wider jaunts, helping both to reduce our environmental impact and to allow the non-drivers among us to fully participate.

Thanks to the publishers listed below for allowing inclusion in this anthology:

Sue Burge's poem *Snow Queen* appeared in the Ink Sweat and Tears *2022 Twelve Days of Christmas* Special Issue. All five of Sue Burge's poems will be included in her forthcoming collection with Yaffle Press *"watch it slowly fade"*.

A number of the items and many others besides, have been included in a series of pamphlets entitled *Inside Writing Outside* which Bob Ward generously produced and gifted to participants.

Jonathan Ward's poems *Patience* and *A Gift* have been published in *Swallows in Late September: New & Selected Poems* (Harwood & Elwood, 2018, expanded edition 2024) and have been displayed in exhibitions at Anteros Arts Foundation in Norwich and St Nicholas Church, Salthouse alongside the work of visual artists.

We would like to offer special thanks to all of the staff and volunteers at the Norfolk Wildlife Trust, especially those working in and around the visitor centre at Cley Marshes, without whom none of this work would exist.